HANDBOOK

for

PRAYING SCRIPTURE

>>>>>><<<<<<

WILLIAM VARNER

featuring the
LEGACY STANDARD BIBLE

EXPLANATION OF GENERAL FORMAT FOR THE LEGACY STANDARD BIBLE

Italics are used in the text to indicate words which are not found in the original Hebrew, Aramaic, or Greek but implied by it.

Small Caps in the New Testament are used in the text to indicate Old Testament quotations or obvious references to OT texts. Variations of OT wording are found in NT citations depending on whether the NT writer translated from a Hebrew text, used existing Greek or Aramaic translations, or paraphrased the material. It should be noted that modern rules for the indication of direct quotation were not used in biblical times; thus, the ancient writer would use exact quotations or references to quotation without specific indication of such.

The complete LSB Foreword can be found at read.LSBible.org.

CONTENTS

PREFACE 7

PROLOGUE 13

PRAYING SCRIPTURE FOR A MONTH 15

PRAYING SCRIPTURE FOR A WEEK 145

APPENDIX ONE
Prayers from Church History 187

APPENDIX TWO
Prayers for Christian Holidays 203

APPENDIX THREE
Prayers for the Christian Life 219

EPILOGUE 247

SCRIPTURE INDEX 249

DEDICATION

My books have been dedicated to individuals who have influenced me in various ways. When I considered to whom I should dedicate this book of Scripture prayers, I cannot think of anyone else but the One who made this all possible by saving a Southern boy over fifty-eight years ago and giving me the marvelous privilege of ministering His truth to others.

> Now to the King of the ages, immortal,
> invisible, the only God, *be* honor and
> glory forever and ever. Amen. *(1 Tim 1:17)*

And also to my hero, James, the brother of the Lord, and a giant of prayer.

> Therefore, confess your sins to one
> another, and pray for one another so that
> you may be healed. The effective prayer
> of a righteous man can accomplish much.
> *(James 5:16)*

Years ago I was struggling to stay focused during my private times of prayer. As hard as I tried, my mind would wander. I was aware of several resources from the liturgical denominations and other Christian traditions, but I did not want to only pray other people's prayers. I desired to pray Scripture. I discovered a few books of prayers drawn largely from Scripture, along with a few other prayer resources, some within the broader Evangelical tradition. Donald Whitney's *Praying the Bible* (Crossway, 2015), Evan Howard's *Praying the Scriptures* (IVP, 1999), and Philip Reinder's *Seeking God's Face: Praying with the Bible through the Year* (Faith Alive, 2013) have all been helpful. The prayer book I have found most refreshing has been *Handbook to Prayer: Praying Scripture Back to God* by Ken Boa (Trinity House Publishers, 1993). Dr. Boa utilizes prayers mostly from the Psalms in a structured pattern for each day over a three-week period with different Scripture selections. He also encourages the reader to "pause" and offer up personal praises and prayers.

One morning as I was praying the Scriptures in Boa's volume of prayers, I had the idea of preparing a new prayer handbook utilizing Scripture from the *Legacy Standard Bible* (*LSB*). As I continued exploring the framework for such a handbook, I decided it would first include a guide for **Praying Scripture for a Month** consisting of 31 daily sets of prayers utilizing Scripture. This monthly guide can then be repeated in successive months. The second part is a more in-depth guide for **Praying Scripture for a Week** consisting of seven daily sets of prayers with the same structure but utilizing more Scripture. Passages rather than individual verses are the emphasis in the weekly guide, which can be utilized during other times of day or simply when one desires a more in-depth time of prayer.

One Scripture prayer that is intended to be prayed every day is what is often referred to as "The Lord's Prayer." What is *really* the "Lord's Prayer" is found in John 17, because it is His prayer to His Father on the way to Gethsemane. The way He taught His *disciples* to pray is found in Matthew 6:9-13 and I refer to it, therefore, as the "Disciples' Prayer." An early Christian writing called the Didache encourages believers to pray this prayer three times a day, so I also encourage you to pray it at least once daily! This *Handbook* also includes some added affirmations like the Apostles' and Nicene Creeds and the Ten Commandments, as well as a few favorite prayers of mine that are not direct quotations of Scripture.

This *Handbook for Praying Scripture*, more than any book I have written, comes out of my own personal walk with the Lord. Early in my Christian walk, a youth speaker encouraged us to have an "A.C.T.S. Prayer Meeting." What he meant by that acronym was that all prayers should consist of Adoration, Confession, Thanksgiving, and Supplication. This is a helpful guide, which I have adapted and expanded to include Affirmation and Benediction. I have partitioned Supplication into two elements: Petition (for oneself) and Intercession (for others). The daily prayers in this *Handbook* will follow the regular pattern of beginning with the more positive prayers of **Adoration** and **Thanksgiving**, followed by the realistic needs of personal **Confession**, and continue with **Affirmation**, the **Disciples' Prayer**, **Petition**, **Intercession**, closing with a **Benediction**. There are reasons for this order. Worship of God, thanksgiving to Him, confession of sins, and affirmation of His attributes (the upward focus) should precede personal requests and intercessions (the inner and outer focus). It works for me to focus on the Lord first, then people, and I pray that this order will for you too. The "Pause" after each element encourages the praying Christian to add any personal praises or petitions that are on their heart and mind.

Martin Luther wrote that he always included three elements in his daily prayers: praying the Lord's (Disciples') Prayer, affirming the Apostles' Creed, and reciting the Ten Commandments. I have found that by doing likewise I follow our Lord's command in regards to His model in the Disciples' Prayer, and am reminded daily of what I should believe, as well as what I should and should not do. Therefore, I include both the Apostles' and the Nicene Creeds as well as the Ten Commandments in **Appendix One**. This is where you will also find a few of my favorite prayers. **Appendix Two** includes Scripture over which to pray and meditate during annual Christian holidays and seasons. **Appendix Three** recommends Scripture to ponder and pray over throughout our daily Christian walk and ministry. Each of these Biblical texts can easily be turned into prayer!

Since this *Handbook* is a reflection of many of my own prayer practices, I have always included Psalm 139:23-24 and Psalm 19:14 at the end of each of the daily Confession and Affirmation sections. The benefit of daily praying these specific Scriptures is that they will hopefully become part of our memory banks and embedded into our hearts and souls. You may also have some of your own prayer practices. Therefore two lined pages have been placed at the end of each section for you to add your favorite prayers or Scriptures to this *Handbook*.

I had the inestimable privilege to be part of the team who translated the *Legacy Standard Bible*. Therefore, I utilize Scripture from the *LSB*, and I personally have found that it reinvigorates my prayers to address God by His personal name, Yahweh (Ex 3:13-15). While the Psalms and prayers that are addressed directly to Yahweh are in most instances reproduced as they are written in the *LSB*, I occasionally adapt a text to a second-person address to God or a first-person affirmation while still maintaining the wording as much as possible. These minor changes are noted in the Scripture reference with a marker (e.g., ⁺Heb 13:2). No prayer using Scripture is ever altered in its meaning.

The observant reader may remember my earlier hesitance to depend on a prayer book that consists of other people's prayers. Then one might ask how are other people's prayers from Scripture any different? I suggest that praying *inspired* prayers from the canon of sacred texts is different from praying otherwise excellent prayers. Many of the prayers in this collection were originally prayers uttered by Biblical authors! What better prayers can there be?

I would like to thank a layman who has provided a great example to me of what prayer should look like in a believer's life. I thank the Lord for His grace in the prayerful example of this dear friend and brother who can just be called Fred. Other co-workers in the ministry have also graciously reviewed this *Handbook.* I also wish to thank a faculty colleague, Ruta Bloomfield, for making a very good suggestion about the phrasing of the personal "pause prayer requests" that I have followed. My wife of over fifty years, Helen, also sympathetically reviewed this collection of prayers and helped with the Scripture Index. Thanks also to Megan Smith for her careful proofreading. A special *thank you* goes to the nearly five thousand members of the Legacy Standard Bible Fan Group on Facebook who have encouraged me through their lively interest in this new translation of the Bible and especially in this project.

Finally, I wrestled with the idea of including the following deeply personal reason why praying Scripture has become very important to me. I include it now with the prayer that it will be helpful to the reader. In 2005 our twenty-six year-old daughter, Lynda Joy, died in an automobile accident. Some have asked what got me through that awful experience. My brief answer relates to the subject of this book. I do not want to oversimplify my experience, but Job's statements in chapters one and two of his book helped me through the awful shock of that first week. Among those amazing statements are: "Naked I came from my mother's womb, and naked I shall return there. Yahweh gave, and Yahweh has taken away. Blessed be the name of Yahweh" (Job 1:21). Job's amazing responses, not simply recited by me coldly without feeling, sustained me then and they still do today. I have chosen to focus not on my loss but on the years that my precious daughter was with us. It was actually soon after her death that I began the practice of praying Scripture. It kept my prayer life focused and it still does today. May it do the same for you, whatever your specific circumstances might be.

PROLOGUE

Your words were found, and I ate them,
And Your words became for me joy
    and gladness in my heart,
For I have been called by Your name,
O Yahweh God of hosts. *(Jer 15:16)*

The experience of praying the Scriptures can be likened to the experience of "feasting on the Word." First, one takes a bite (reading the Word); then one chews it (meditating on the Word); then one savors its essence (praying the Word); and, finally, one digests the food and makes it a part of the body (obeying the Word).

It is my hope and prayer that this *Handbook for Praying Scripture* will help many to feast on the Word of God and not to be satisfied with only tasting it!

PRAYING SCRIPTURE

FOR A MONTH

DAY 1

ADORATION
Ps 34:1-3

I will bless Yahweh at all times;
His praise shall continually be in my mouth.
My soul will make its boast in Yahweh;
The humble will hear it and rejoice.
O magnify Yahweh with me,
And let us exalt His name together.

Ps 94:22

But Yahweh has been my stronghold,
And my God the rock of my refuge.

↵ **Pause to bless God and boast about His attributes**

THANKSGIVING
1 Chr 16:34

Oh give thanks to Yahweh, for He is good,
For His lovingkindness endures forever.

2 Cor 2:14

But thanks be to God, who always leads us
in triumphal procession in Christ, and manifests
through us the aroma of the knowledge of Him
in every place.

↵ **Pause to give thanks to your God for specific tokens
of His kindness**

All the paths of Yahweh are lovingkindness
    and truth
To those who guard His covenant
    and His testimonies.
For Your name's sake, O Yahweh,
Pardon my iniquity, for it is great.

Ps 139:23-24 Search me, O God, and know my heart;
Try me and know my anxious thoughts;
And see if there be any hurtful way in me,
And lead me in the everlasting way.

↙ **Pause to confess to God any specific sins that are bothering you**

AFFIRMATION Yahweh is my God, Yahweh is one!
⁺Deut 6:4-5 I will love Yahweh my God with all my heart
and with all my soul and with all my might.

Is 55:11 So will My word be which goes forth
    from My mouth;
It will not return to Me empty,
Without accomplishing what pleases Me,
And without succeeding *in the matter*
    for which I sent it.

↙ **Pause to affirm the certainty of God's promises**

DISCIPLES'
PRAYER
Matt 6:9b-13
Our Father who is in heaven,
Hallowed be Your name.
Your kingdom come. Your will be done,
On earth as it is in heaven.
Give us this day our daily bread.
And forgive us our debts,
    as we also have forgiven our debtors.
And do not lead us into temptation
    but deliver us from the evil one.
For Yours is the kingdom and the power
    and the glory forever. Amen.

✍ **Pause to recognize that although God is in heaven He can still be addressed as your Father**

PETITION
⁺Col 4:5-6
May I walk in wisdom toward outsiders, redeeming the time. Let my words always be with grace, seasoned with salt, so that I will know how I should answer each person.

Ps 19:14
Let the words of my mouth
    and the meditation of my heart
Be acceptable in Your sight,
O Yahweh, my rock and my Redeemer.

✍ **Pause to ask God to help you in your relationships with unbelievers**

Turn us back, O God of our salvation,
And cause Your vexation toward us to cease.
Will You be angry with us forever?
Will You prolong Your anger from generation
    to generation?
Will You not Yourself return to revive us,
That Your people may be glad in You?
Show us, O Yahweh, Your lovingkindness,
And give us Your salvation.

🔽 **Pause to intercede with God for renewal among His people**

Now the God of peace, who brought up from the dead the great Shepherd of the sheep through the blood of the eternal covenant, our Lord Jesus, equip us in every good thing to do His will, by doing in us what is pleasing in His sight, through Jesus Christ, to whom *be* the glory forever and ever. Amen.

DAY 2

O Lord, Your servant John heard the following from heaven: "Hallelujah! For the Lord our God, the Almighty, reigns. Let us rejoice and be glad and give the glory to Him, for the marriage of the Lamb has come and His bride has made herself ready." "Write, 'Blessed are those who are invited to the marriage supper of the Lamb.'" And he said to me, "These are true words of God."

Rev 22:16b Lord Jesus, You are the root and the descendant of David, the bright morning star.

📖 Pause to adore your God for the certainty of His promises about the future

THANKSGIVING
*Ps 118:25-
27a, 28-29*

O Yahweh, save! O Yahweh, succeed!
Blessed is the one who comes in the name
    of Yahweh;
We have blessed you from the house of Yahweh.
Yahweh is God, and He has given us light;
You are my God, and I give thanks to You;
You are my God, I exalt You.
Give thanks to Yahweh, for He is good;
For His lovingkindness endures forever.

📖 Pause to give thanks to God for specific examples of His kindness

How blessed is he whose transgression is forgiven,
Whose sin is covered!
How blessed is the man whose iniquity
    Yahweh will not take into account,
And in whose spirit there is no deceit!
When I kept silent *about my sin*,
    my bones wasted away
Through my groaning all day long.
For day and night Your hand was heavy upon me;
My vitality was drained away
    as with the heat of summer.   Selah.
I acknowledged my sin to You,
And my iniquity I did not cover up;
I said, "I will confess my transgressions
    to Yahweh;"
And You forgave the iniquity of my sin.   Selah.

Ps 139:23-24

Search me, O God, and know my heart;
Try me and know my anxious thoughts;
And see if there be any hurtful way in me,
And lead me in the everlasting way.

🐾 **Pause to confess to God any specific sins that you know about**

AFFIRMATION
Ps 119:162-168

I rejoice at Your word,
As one who finds much spoil.
I hate and abhor lying,
But I love Your law.
Seven times a day I praise You,
Because of Your righteous judgments.

Those who love Your law have much peace,
And nothing causes them to stumble.
I hope for Your salvation, O Yahweh,
And I do Your commandments.
My soul keeps Your testimonies,
And I love them exceedingly.
I keep Your precepts and Your testimonies,
For all my ways are before You.

〴 **Pause to affirm God's truth**

DISCIPLES' Our Father who is in heaven,
PRAYER Hallowed be Your name.
Matt 6:9b-13 Your kingdom come. Your will be done,
On earth as it is in heaven.
Give us this day our daily bread.
And forgive us our debts,
 as we also have forgiven our debtors.
And do not lead us into temptation
 but deliver us from the evil one.
For Yours is the kingdom and the power
 and the glory forever. Amen.

〴 **Pause to recognize that your Father's "name" is more
than a title but embodies all that He is**

PETITION May I fight the good fight, may I finish my
+2 Tim 4:7-8 course, may I keep the faith. In the future there
is laid up for me the crown of righteousness,
which the Lord, the righteous Judge, will award

to me on that day, and not only to me, but also to all who have loved His appearing.

Ps 19:14 Let the words of my mouth
          and the meditation of my heart
          Be acceptable in Your sight,
          O Yahweh, my rock and my Redeemer.

🍂 **Pause to ask God about your personal needs**

INTERCESSION Whatever prayer or supplication is made by
2 Chr 6:29- any man or by all Your people Israel, who know
31a his own affliction and his own pain, and spread
     his hands toward this house, then listen from
     heaven Your dwelling place, and forgive, and
     give to each according to all his ways, whose
     heart You know, for You alone know the hearts
     of the sons of men, that they may fear You, to
     walk in Your ways all the days they live.

🍂 **Pause to intercede with God for others, especially pastors
    and Christian workers**

BENEDICTION Now to Him who is able to keep us from
⁺Jude 24-25 stumbling, and to make us stand in the presence
     of His glory blameless with great joy, to the only
     God our Savior, through Jesus Christ our Lord,
     be glory, majesty, might, and authority, before
     all time and now and forever. Amen.

ADORATION
Amos 4:13

For behold, He who forms mountains
   and creates the wind
And declares to man what are His thoughts.
He who makes dawn into gloom
And treads on the high places of the earth,
Yahweh God of hosts is His name.

꒰ **Pause to behold your God seven times today**

THANKSGIVING
Ps 89:1-2

I will sing of the lovingkindnesses
   of Yahweh forever;
From generation to generation I will make
   known Your faithfulness with my mouth.
For I have said, "Lovingkindness
   will be built up forever;
In the heavens You will establish
   Your faithfulness."

꒰ **Pause to give thanks to God for specific tokens
of His faithfulness**

CONFESSION
Ps 25:6-11

Remember, O Yahweh, Your compassion
   and Your lovingkindnesses,
For they have been from of old.
Do not remember the sins of my youth
   or my transgressions;

According to Your lovingkindness remember me,
For the sake of Your goodness, O Yahweh.
Good and upright is Yahweh;
Therefore He instructs sinners in the way.
May He lead the humble in justice,
And may He teach the humble His way.
All the paths of Yahweh are lovingkindness
    and truth
To those who guard His covenant
    and His testimonies.
For Your name's sake, O Yahweh,
Pardon my iniquity, for it is great.

Ps 139:23-24   Search me, O God, and know my heart;
Try me and know my anxious thoughts;
And see if there be any hurtful way in me,
And lead me in the everlasting way.

᷍   **Pause to confess to God when you have taken for granted
His lovingkindness**

AFFIRMATION   As for me, I shall call upon God,
Ps 55:16-17   And Yahweh will save me.
Evening and morning and at noon,
I will bring my complaint and moan,
And He will hear my voice.

'Eph 2:19-22   Lord, I am no longer a stranger and a sojourner,
but I am a fellow citizen with the saints, and
am of God's household, having been built on the

foundation of the apostles and prophets,
Christ Jesus Himself being the corner *stone*.
In whom the whole building, being joined
together, is growing into a holy sanctuary
in the Lord; in whom I also am being built
together into a dwelling of God in the Spirit.

✍ **Pause to affirm your place in His family**

DISCIPLES' Our Father who is in heaven,
PRAYER Hallowed be Your name.
Matt 6:9b-13 Your kingdom come. Your will be done,
On earth as it is in heaven.
Give us this day our daily bread.
And forgive us our debts,
as we also have forgiven our debtors.
And do not lead us into temptation
but deliver us from the evil one.
For Yours is the kingdom and the power
and the glory forever. Amen.

✍ **Pause to recognize how God's kingdom is both now and also yet to come**

PETITION May no unwholesome word proceed from
†Eph 4:29-32 my mouth, but only such *a word* as is good for
building up what is needed, so that it will give
grace to those who hear. And may I not grieve
the Holy Spirit of God, by whom I was sealed
for the day of redemption. May all bitterness

and anger and wrath and shouting and slander
be put away from me, along with all malice.
Instead, may I be kind to others, tender-hearted,
graciously forgiving others, just as God in Christ
also has graciously forgiven me.

Ps 19:14 Let the words of my mouth
and the meditation of my heart
Be acceptable in Your sight,
O Yahweh, my rock and my Redeemer.

🕊 **Pause to ask your gracious God about attitudinal sins**

INTERCESSION I devote myself to prayer, being watchful in it
†Col 4:2-4 with thanksgiving; praying at the same time
that God will open up to me a door for the word,
so that I may speak the mystery of Christ,
for which I may also be bound, that I may make it
manifest in the way I ought to speak.

🕊 **Pause to intercede with God to open doors for your
witness to others**

BENEDICTION May Yahweh bless us, and keep us;
†Num 6:24-26 May Yahweh make His face shine on us,
And be gracious to us;
May Yahweh lift up His face on us,
And give us peace.

ADORATION
Ps 103:20-22

Bless Yahweh, you His angels,
Mighty in strength, who perform His word,
Obeying the voice of His word!
Bless Yahweh, all you His hosts,
You who serve Him, doing His will.
Bless Yahweh, all you works of His,
In all places of His rule;
Bless Yahweh, O my soul!

↙ Pause to simply adore your God—"O come let us adore Him"

THANKSGIVING
2 Cor 5:9-10

Therefore we also have as our ambition,
whether at home or absent, to be pleasing to Him.
For we must all appear before the judgment seat
of Christ, so that each one may be recompensed
for his deeds in the body, according to what he
has done, whether good or bad.

↙ Pause to thank God for holding you accountable!

CONFESSION
⁺Ps 4:1, 4-5

Answer me when I call,
O God of my righteousness!
You have relieved me in my distress;
Be gracious to me and hear my prayer.
I tremble, but I do not sin;

I ponder in my heart upon my bed and I am still.

Selah.

I offer the sacrifices of righteousness,
And I trust in Yahweh.

Ps 139:23-24 Search me, O God, and know my heart;
Try me and know my anxious thoughts;
And see if there be any hurtful way in me,
And lead me in the everlasting way.

🖋 **Pause to confess to God sins of the heart**

AFFIRMATION As for me, I shall call upon God,
⁺Ps 55:16-17, 22 And Yahweh will save me.
Evening and morning and at noon,
I will bring my complaint and moan,
And He will hear my voice.
I will cast my burden upon Yahweh
and He will sustain me;
He will never allow the righteous to be shaken.

Is 57:15 For thus says the One high and lifted up
Who dwells forever, whose name is Holy,
"I dwell on a high and holy place,
And also with the crushed and lowly of spirit
In order to revive the spirit of the lowly
And to revive the heart of the crushed."

🖋 **Pause to thank Him that in Jesus He is both high and holy and meek and lowly**

Our Father who is in heaven,
Hallowed be Your name.
Your kingdom come. Your will be done,
On earth as it is in heaven.
Give us this day our daily bread.
And forgive us our debts,
    as we also have forgiven our debtors.
And do not lead us into temptation
    but deliver us from the evil one.
For Yours is the kingdom and the power
    and the glory forever. Amen.

✒ **Pause to delight in your Father's will in whatever way it is being shown to you**

May I and my fellow believers be like-minded, sympathetic, brotherly, tender-hearted, and humble in spirit; not returning evil for evil or reviling for reviling, but giving a blessing instead, for we were called for the very purpose that we might inherit a blessing.

Ps 19:14 Let the words of my mouth
    and the meditation of my heart
Be acceptable in Your sight,
O Yahweh, my rock and my Redeemer.

✒ **Pause to ask God to keep you honest before your brothers and sisters**

*2 Thess
2:16-17

Now may our Lord Jesus Christ Himself and God our Father, who has loved us and given us eternal comfort and good hope by grace, encourage our hearts and strengthen them in every good work and word.

↲ **Pause to intercede with God to make you an encourager of others**

BENEDICTION
*1 Kin 8:56-60

Blessed be Yahweh, who has given rest to His people, according to all that He promised; not one promise has failed of all His good promises, which He promised by the hand of Moses His servant. May Yahweh our God be with us, as He was with our fathers; may He not forsake us or abandon us, that He may incline our hearts to Himself, to walk in all His ways and to keep His commandments and His statutes and His judgments, which He commanded our fathers. And may these words of mine, with which I have made supplication before Yahweh, be near to Yahweh our God day and night, that He may do justice for His slave and justice for His people, as each day requires, so that all the peoples of the earth may know that Yahweh is God; there is no one else.

ADORATION
Ps 150:1-2, 6

Praise Yah! Praise God in His sanctuary;
Praise Him in His mighty expanse.
Praise Him for His mighty deeds;
Praise Him according to the abundance
    of His greatness.
Let everything that has breath praise Yah.
Praise Yah!

  🖰 **Pause to behold your God**

THANKSGIVING
⁺Jer 31:3

Yahweh appeared to me from afar, saying,
"I have loved you with an everlasting love;
Therefore I have drawn you with lovingkindness."

⁺1 Thess 5:18

In everything I will give thanks, for this is God's
will for me in Christ Jesus.

  🖰 **Pause to give thanks to God for tokens of His kindness
to you**

CONFESSION
⁺Dan 9:7, 17

To You, O Lord, belongs righteousness, but to
me open shame, as it is this day—because of
my unfaithful deeds which I have committed
against You. So now, my God, listen to the
prayer of Your slave and to his supplications,
and for Your sake, O Lord, let Your face shine
on me again.

Ps 139:23-24 Search me, O God, and know my heart;
Try me and know my anxious thoughts;
And see if there be any hurtful way in me,
And lead me in the everlasting way.

📖 **Pause to confess to God any inappropriate thoughts**

AFFIRMATION Oh how I love Your law!
Ps 119:97 It is my meditation all the day.

⁺2 Tim 3:16-17 All Scripture is God-breathed and profitable
for teaching, for reproof, for correction, for
training in righteousness, so that I may be
thoroughly equipped for every good work.

Rom 15:4 For whatever was written in earlier times was
written for our instruction, so that through the
perseverance and the encouragement of the
Scriptures we might have hope.

📖 **Pause to affirm God's truth as it is conveyed in His Word**

DISCIPLES' Our Father who is in heaven,
PRAYER Hallowed be Your name.
Matt 6:9b-13 Your kingdom come. Your will be done,
On earth as it is in heaven.
Give us this day our daily bread.
And forgive us our debts,
    as we also have forgiven our debtors.

And do not lead us into temptation
  but deliver us from the evil one.
For Yours is the kingdom and the power
  and the glory forever. Amen.

📖 **Pause to reflect on how your Father's will in heaven can be realized on earth**

PETITION
Ps 16:1-3, 5-6

Keep me, O God, for I take refuge in You.
O my soul, you have said to Yahweh,
"You are my Lord;
I have no good without You."
As for the saints who are in the earth,
They are the majestic ones in whom
  is all my delight.
Yahweh is the portion of my inheritance
  and my cup;
You support my lot.
The lines have fallen to me in pleasant places;
Indeed, my inheritance is beautiful to me.

Ps 19:14

Let the words of my mouth
  and the meditation of my heart
Be acceptable in Your sight,
O Yahweh, my rock and my Redeemer.

📖 **Pause to ask God for support in your endeavors**

INTERCESSION

⁺1 Tim 2:1-3 First of all, then, I offer petitions and prayers, requests and thanksgivings, for all men, for kings and all who are in authority, so that I may lead a tranquil and quiet life in all godliness and dignity. This is good and acceptable in the sight of God our Savior, who desires all men to be saved and to come to the full knowledge of the truth.

🖎 **Pause to intercede with God for the unsaved**

BENEDICTION

Ps 72:18-19 Blessed be Yahweh God, the God of Israel,
Who alone works wondrous deeds.
And blessed be His glorious name forever;
And may the whole earth be filled with His glory.
Amen, and Amen.

DAY 6

ADORATION
†Ps 42:1-2, 5

As the deer pants for the water brooks,
So my soul pants for You, O God.
My soul thirsts for God, for the living God;
When shall I come and appear before God?
Why are you in despair, O my soul?
And why are you disturbed within me?
I will wait for God, for I shall still praise Him,
For the salvation of Your presence.

↙ **Pause to adore your God and wait for Him**

THANKSGIVING
Ps 40:1-3

I hoped earnestly for Yahweh;
And He inclined to me and heard my cry
     for help.
He brought me up out of the pit of destruction,
     out of the miry clay,
And He set my feet upon a high rock,
He established my steps.
He put a new song in my mouth,
     a song of praise to our God;
Many will see and fear
And will trust in Yahweh.

↙ **Pause to give thanks to God for stability and joy**

CONFESSION "Draw near to God and He will draw near to you.
James 4:8-10 Cleanse your hands, you sinners, and purify
your hearts, you double-minded. Be miserable
and mourn and cry. Let your laughter be turned
into mourning and your joy to gloom. Humble
yourselves in the presence of the Lord, and He
will exalt you." Lord, I will heed this call from
James and humble myself before You.

Ps 139:23-24 Search me, O God, and know my heart;
Try me and know my anxious thoughts;
And see if there be any hurtful way in me,
And lead me in the everlasting way.

🍃 Pause to confess to God any remnants of pride in your heart

AFFIRMATION I have as more sure the prophetic word, to which
2 Pet 1:19-21 I do well to pay attention as to a lamp shining in
a dark place, until the day dawns and the morning
star arises in my heart. Because I know this first
of all, that no prophecy of Scripture comes by
one's own interpretation. For no prophecy was
ever made by the will of man, but men being
moved by the Holy Spirit spoke from God.

🍃 Pause to affirm the certainty of God's truth

DISCIPLES' Our Father who is in heaven,
PRAYER Hallowed be Your name.
Matt 6:9b-13 Your kingdom come. Your will be done,

On earth as it is in heaven.
Give us this day our daily bread.
And forgive us our debts,
    as we also have forgiven our debtors.
And do not lead us into temptation
    but deliver us from the evil one.
For Yours is the kingdom and the power
    and the glory forever. Amen.

📖 **Pause to be grateful for Israel's daily manna and your daily food**

PETITION
Ps 25:20-21

Keep my soul and deliver me;
Do not let me be ashamed,
    for I take refuge in You.
Let integrity and uprightness guard me,
For I hope in You.

Ps 31:1-5

In You, O Yahweh, I have taken refuge;
Let me never be ashamed;
In Your righteousness protect me.
Incline Your ear to me, deliver me quickly;
Be to me a rock of strength,
A fortress to save me.
For You are my high rock and my fortress;
For Your name's sake You will lead me
    and guide me.
You will bring me out of the net
    which they have secretly laid for me,

For You are my strength.
Into Your hand I commit my spirit;
You have ransomed me, O Yahweh, God of truth.

Ps 19:14 Let the words of my mouth
and the meditation of my heart
Be acceptable in Your sight,
O Yahweh, my rock and my Redeemer.

🖋 **Pause to ask God to keep you honest in your relationship with others**

INTERCESSION
⁺*Heb 13:2* May I not neglect to show hospitality to strangers, for by this some have entertained angels without knowing it.

⁺*Heb 13:3* Lord, I remember the prisoners, as though in prison with them, and those who are mistreated, since I myself also am in the body.

🖋 **Pause to intercede with God for prisoners and others who are mistreated**

BENEDICTION
⁺*2 Cor 13:14* May the grace of the Lord Jesus Christ, and the love of God, and the fellowship of the Holy Spirit, be with us all. Amen.

ADORATION
Ps 63:1-4

O God, You are my God; I shall seek You earnestly;
My soul thirsts for You, my flesh yearns for You,
In a dry and weary land without water.
Thus I have beheld You in the sanctuary,
To see Your power and Your glory.
Because Your lovingkindness is better than life,
My lips will laud You.
Thus I will bless You as long as I live;
I will lift up my hands in Your name.

🍃 **Pause to adore your God even in your desert experiences**

THANKSGIVING
Ps 34:6-7

This poor man called out, and Yahweh
 heard him
And saved him out of all his troubles.
The angel of Yahweh encamps
 around those who fear Him,
And rescues them.

🍃 **Pause to give thanks to God for rescuing you from your own foolishness**

CONFESSION
1 John 1:8-9

If we say that we have no sin, we deceive
ourselves and the truth is not in us. If we
confess our sins, He is faithful and righteous
to forgive us our sins and to cleanse us from
all unrighteousness.

Ps 139:23-24   Search me, O God, and know my heart;
Try me and know my anxious thoughts;
And see if there be any hurtful way in me,
And lead me in the everlasting way.

↳ **Pause to confess to God specific sins that are being revealed to you**

AFFIRMATION   For His dominion is an everlasting dominion,
Dan 4:34b-35   And His kingdom *endures* from generation
to generation.
And all the inhabitants of the earth
are accounted as nothing,
But He does according to His will in the host
of heaven
And *among* the inhabitants of earth;
And no one can strike against His hand
Or say to Him, "What have You done?"

Acts 17:24-25   The God who made the world and all things
in it, since He is Lord of heaven and earth,
does not dwell in temples made with hands;
nor is He served by human hands, as though
He needed anything, since He Himself gives
to all *people* life and breath and all things.

↳ **Pause to affirm God's sovereignty over His creation and in your life**

Our Father who is in heaven,
Hallowed be Your name.
Matt 6:9b-13 Your kingdom come. Your will be done,
On earth as it is in heaven.
Give us this day our daily bread.
And forgive us our debts,
as we also have forgiven our debtors.
And do not lead us into temptation
but deliver us from the evil one.
For Yours is the kingdom and the power
and the glory forever. Amen.

🖎 **Pause to decide how you can show to others the Father's mercy shown to you**

PETITION Whatever I do, may I do Your work heartily,
†Col 3:23-24 as for the Lord rather than for men, knowing
that from the Lord I will receive the reward of
the inheritance, because I serve the Lord Christ.

Ps 19:14 Let the words of my mouth
and the meditation of my heart
Be acceptable in Your sight,
O Yahweh, my rock and my Redeemer.

🖎 **Pause to ask God to make you a hearty follower of His work**

Salvation belongs to Yahweh;

Ps 3:8 Your blessing be upon Your people!   Selah.

†Heb 13:16 May I not neglect doing good and sharing,
for with such sacrifices God is pleased.

✍ **Pause to intercede with God for blessings on your fellow
believers**

BENEDICTION May Yahweh bless us, and keep us;

†Num 6:24-26 May Yahweh make His face shine on us,
And be gracious to us;
May Yahweh lift up His face on us,
And give us peace.

DAY 8

"Worthy is the Lamb that was slain to receive power and riches and wisdom and strength and honor and glory and blessing." And every created thing which is in heaven and on the earth and under the earth and on the sea, and all things in them, I heard saying, "To Him who sits on the throne, and to the Lamb, *be* the blessing and the honor and the glory and the might forever and ever."

🕊 **Pause to adore God in your barren times**

Yahweh has established His throne
   in the heavens,
And His kingdom rules over all.
Bless Yahweh, you His angels,
Mighty in strength, who perform His word,
Obeying the voice of His word!
Bless Yahweh, all *you* His hosts,
You who serve Him, doing His will.
Bless Yahweh, all you works of His,
In all places of His rule;
Bless Yahweh, O my soul!

🕊 **Pause to give thanks to God for creation and His powerful acts**

I know that You are a gracious and
compassionate God, slow to anger and
abundant in lovingkindness, and one
who relents concerning evil.

Ps 139:23-24   Search me, O God, and know my heart;
Try me and know my anxious thoughts;
And see if there be any hurtful way in me,
And lead me in the everlasting way.

↙ **Pause to confess to God those times when you are
not gracious**

Though the fig tree should not blossom
Hab 3:17-19a   And there be no produce on the vines,
Though the yield of the olive should fail
And the fields yield no food,
Though the flock should be cut off
from the fold
And there be no cattle in the stalls,
Yet I will exult in Yahweh;
I will rejoice in the God of my salvation.
Yahweh, the Lord, is my strength,
And He has set my feet like hinds' *feet*
And makes me tread on my high places.

↙ **Pause to affirm God's faithfulness even in the hard times**

Our Father who is in heaven,
Hallowed be Your name.
Your kingdom come. Your will be done,
On earth as it is in heaven.
Give us this day our daily bread.
And forgive us our debts,
  as we also have forgiven our debtors.
And do not lead us into temptation
  but deliver us from the evil one.
For Yours is the kingdom and the power
  and the glory forever. Amen.

✍ **Pause to prepare your spiritual armor so you can resist the devil's schemes**

PETITION
Job 14:14
If a man dies, will he live *again*?
All the days of my labor I will wait
Until my change comes.

Gal 6:14
But may it never be that I would boast,
except in the cross of our Lord Jesus Christ,
through which the world has been crucified
to me, and I to the world.

Ps 19:14
Let the words of my mouth
  and the meditation of my heart
Be acceptable in Your sight,
O Yahweh, my rock and my Redeemer.

✍ **Pause to ask God to keep you patient and humble**

INTERCESSION

⁺Rom 10:1-3

My heart's desire and my prayer to God for Israel is for their salvation. For I testify about them that they have a zeal for God, but not according to knowledge. For not knowing about the righteousness of God and seeking to establish their own, they do not subject themselves to the righteousness of God.

✍ **Pause to intercede with God for the Jewish people**

BENEDICTION

⁺Heb 13:20-21

Now the God of peace, who brought up from the dead the great Shepherd of the sheep through the blood of the eternal covenant, our Lord Jesus, equip us in every good thing to do His will, by doing in us what is pleasing in His sight, through Jesus Christ, to whom be the glory forever and ever. Amen.

ADORATION
Ps 139:1-6

O Yahweh, You have searched me
and known *me.*
You know when I sit down and when I rise up;
You understand my thought from afar.
You scrutinize my path and my lying down,
And are intimately acquainted
with all my ways.
Even before there is a word on my tongue,
Behold, O Yahweh, You know it all.
You have enclosed me behind and before,
And You have put Your hand upon me.
Such knowledge is too wonderful for me;
It is too high, I cannot attain to it.

↳ **Pause to behold your God**

THANKSGIVING
Is 12:4-5

And in that day you will say,
"Give thanks to Yahweh, call on His name.
Make known His deeds among the peoples;
Make *them* remember that His name is exalted."
Praise Yahweh in song, for He
has done majestic things;
Let this be known throughout the earth.

↳ **Pause to give thanks to God for His mighty creation**

CONFESSION

Ps 25:6-11

Remember, O Yahweh, Your compassion
and Your lovingkindnesses,
For they have been from of old.
Do not remember the sins of my youth
or my transgressions;
According to Your lovingkindness
remember me,
For the sake of Your goodness, O Yahweh.
Good and upright is Yahweh;
Therefore He instructs sinners in the way.
May He lead the humble in justice,
And may He teach the humble His way.
All the paths of Yahweh are lovingkindness
and truth
To those who guard His covenant
and His testimonies.
For Your name's sake, O Yahweh,
Pardon my iniquity, for it is great.

Ps 139:23-24

Search me, O God, and know my heart;
Try me and know my anxious thoughts;
And see if there be any hurtful way in me,
And lead me in the everlasting way.

🖎 **Pause to confess to God any pride and self-sufficiency**

AFFIRMATION

Ps 18:30-32

As for God, His way is blameless;
The word of Yahweh is tried;
He is a shield to all who take refuge in Him.
For who is God, but Yahweh?

And who is a rock, except our God,
The God who girds me with strength
And makes my way blameless?

🍂 **Pause to affirm the certainty of God's truth**

DISCIPLES'
PRAYER
Matt 6:9b-13 Our Father who is in heaven,
Hallowed be Your name.
Your kingdom come. Your will be done,
On earth as it is in heaven.
Give us this day our daily bread.
And forgive us our debts,
    as we also have forgiven our debtors.
And do not lead us into temptation
    but deliver us from the evil one.
For Yours is the kingdom and the power
    and the glory forever. Amen.

🍂 **Pause to meditate on the glorious power of the Father's kingdom**

PETITION
Ps 5:1-3 Give ear to my words, O Yahweh,
Consider my meditation.
Give heed to the sound of my cry for help,
    my King and my God,
For to You I pray.
O Yahweh, in the morning, You will hear
    my voice;
In the morning I will order *my prayer* to You
    and *eagerly* watch.

Ps 19:14   Let the words of my mouth
             and the meditation of my heart
         Be acceptable in Your sight,
         O Yahweh, my rock and my Redeemer.

   ↙ **Pause to ask God about any personal needs**

INTERCESSION   For all of us have become like one who is unclean,
Is 64:6-7a, 8   And all our righteous deeds are like
             a filthy garment;
         And all of us wither like a leaf,
         And our iniquities, like the wind, carry us away.
         There is no one who calls on Your name,
         But now, O Yahweh, You are our Father;
         We are the clay, and You our potter;
         And all of us are the work of Your hand.

   ↙ **Pause to intercede with God for others**

BENEDICTION   O Yahweh, Your name is everlasting,
Ps 135:13,   O Yahweh, Your remembrance is from generation
20b-21   to generation.
         You who fear Yahweh, bless Yahweh.
         Blessed be Yahweh from Zion,
         Who dwells in Jerusalem.
         Praise Yah!

ADORATION Where can I go from Your Spirit?

Ps 139:7-12 Or where can I flee from Your presence?
If I ascend to heaven, You are there;
If I make my bed in Sheol, behold, You are there.
If I lift up the wings of the dawn,
If I dwell in the remotest part of the sea,
Even there Your hand will lead me,
And Your right hand will lay hold of me.
If I say, "Surely the darkness will bruise me,
And the light around me will be night,"
Even the darkness is not too dark for You,
And the night is as bright as the day.
Darkness and light are alike *to You.*

🍃 **Pause to adore your God for His omnipresence**

THANKSGIVING Let us give thanks to Yahweh
*Ps 107:8-9   for His lovingkindness,
And for His wondrous deeds to the sons of men!
For He has satisfied the thirsty soul,
And the hungry soul He has filled
    with what is good.

🍃 **Pause to give thanks to God for His wondrous sustenance of our souls and bodies**

CONFESSION Who can discern *his* errors?
Ps 19:12-13   Acquit me of hidden *faults*.
Also keep back Your slave
    from presumptuous *sins*;
Let them not rule over me;
Then I will be blameless,
And I shall be acquitted of great transgression.

Ps 139:23-24 Search me, O God, and know my heart;
Try me and know my anxious thoughts;
And see if there be any hurtful way in me,
And lead me in the everlasting way.

🍃 **Pause to confess to God any unnoticed sins**

AFFIRMATION How blessed is the man who does not walk
Ps 1:1-3   in the counsel of the wicked,
Nor stand in the way of sinners,
Nor sit in the seat of scoffers!
But his delight is in the law of Yahweh,
And in His law he meditates day and night.
And he will be like a tree *firmly* planted
    by streams of water,
Which yields its fruit in its season
And its leaf does not wither;
And in whatever he does, he prospers.

🍃 **Pause to delight in Yahweh's wonderful Word**

Our Father who is in heaven,
Hallowed be Your name.
Your kingdom come. Your will be done,
On earth as it is in heaven.
Give us this day our daily bread.
And forgive us our debts,
    as we also have forgiven our debtors.
And do not lead us into temptation
    but deliver us from the evil one.
For Yours is the kingdom and the power
    and the glory forever. Amen.

✍ **Pause to recognize that although God is in heaven
He can still be addressed as Father**

PETITION
Ps 121:1-3

I will lift up my eyes to the mountains;
From where shall my help come?
My help *comes* from Yahweh,
Who made heaven and earth.
He will not allow your foot to stumble;
He who keeps you will not slumber.

Ps 19:14
Let the words of my mouth
    and the meditation of my heart
Be acceptable in Your sight,
O Yahweh, my rock and my Redeemer.

✍ **Pause to ask God about your personal needs**

INTERCESSION

2 Thess 1:3

I ought always to give thanks to God for other believers and pray that their faith would grow abundantly and that the love of each of them toward one another would increase all the more.

🔉 **Pause to intercede with God for younger believers**

BENEDICTION

Job 9:9-10

To the One who says for the sun not to shine,
And sets a seal upon the stars;
Who alone stretches out the heavens,
And tramples down the waves of the sea;
To the God who makes the Bear, Orion,
    and the Pleiades,
And the chambers of the south;
Who does great things, unsearchable,
And wondrous works, innumerable.

ADORATION
Ps 139:13-16

For You formed my inward parts;
You wove me in my mother's womb.
I will give thanks to You, for I am fearfully
 and wonderfully made;
Wonderful are Your works,
And my soul knows it very well.
My frame was not hidden from You,
When I was made in secret,
And intricately woven in the depths of the earth;
Your eyes have seen my unshaped substance;
And in Your book all of them were written
The days that were formed *for me*,
When as yet there was not one of them.

✑ **Pause to adore your God for His omnipotence**

THANKSGIVING
Ps 5:11-12

But let all who take refuge in You be glad,
Let them ever sing for joy;
And may You shelter them,
That those who love Your name may exult
 in You.
For it is You who blesses the righteous one,
 O Yahweh,
You surround him with favor
 as with a large shield.

✑ **Pause to thank God for specific blessings**

Ezra 9:6, 8 O my God, I am ashamed and humiliated to lift up my face to You, my God, for my iniquities have multiplied above my head and my guilt has become great even to the heavens. But now for a brief moment grace has been shown from Yahweh our God to enlighten my eyes and give me a little reviving in my slavery.

Ps 139:23-24 Search me, O God, and know my heart;
Try me and know my anxious thoughts;
And see if there be any hurtful way in me,
And lead me in the everlasting way.

🖊 **Pause to confess to God any specific sins that are being brought to light**

AFFIRMATION It is a trustworthy saying:
2 Tim 2:11-13 For if we died with Him, we will also live
with Him;
If we endure, we will also reign with Him;
If we will deny Him, He also will deny us;
If we are faithless, He remains faithful,
for He cannot deny Himself.

†1 Pet 1:3-5 Blessed be the God and Father of our Lord Jesus Christ, who according to His great mercy has caused me to be born again to a living hope through the resurrection of Jesus Christ from the dead, to obtain an inheritance incorruptible and undefiled and unfading, having been kept

in heaven for me, one who is protected by the power of God through faith for a salvation ready to be revealed in the last time.

↙ **Pause to affirm God's faithfulness and blessings**

DISCIPLES' PRAYER
Matt 6:9b-13

Our Father who is in heaven,
Hallowed be Your name.
Your kingdom come. Your will be done,
On earth as it is in heaven.
Give us this day our daily bread.
And forgive us our debts,
    as we also have forgiven our debtors.
And do not lead us into temptation
    but deliver us from the evil one.
For Yours is the kingdom and the power
    and the glory forever. Amen.

↙ **Pause to recognize that your Father's "name" is more than a title but embodies all that He is**

PETITION
⁺Phil 2:3-4

May I do nothing from selfish ambition or vain glory, but with humility of mind regard others as more important than myself, not merely looking out for my own personal interests, but also for the interests of others.

Ps 19:14

Let the words of my mouth
    and the meditation of my heart

Be acceptable in Your sight,
O Yahweh, my rock and my Redeemer.

🔖 **Pause to beseech God about others who are needy**

INTERCESSION Yours, O Yahweh, is the greatness and the power
†1 Chr 29:11- and the glory and the victory and the majesty,
13, 18 indeed everything that is in the heavens and the
earth; Yours is the kingdom, O Yahweh, and You
exalt Yourself as head over all. Both riches and
honor come from You, and You rule over all, and
in Your hand is power and might; and it lies in Your
hand to make great and to strengthen everyone. So
now, our God, we are thanking You and praising
Your glorious name. Because of this, O Yahweh,
the God of Abraham, Isaac, and Israel, our fathers,
keep this forever in the intentions of the heart of
Your people, and prepare their heart to You.

🔖 **Pause to intercede with God to strengthen other believers**

BENEDICTION Oh, the depth of the riches and wisdom and
Rom 11:33-36 knowledge of God! How unsearchable are His
judgments and unfathomable His ways! For WHO
HAS KNOWN THE MIND OF THE LORD, OR WHO BECAME
HIS COUNSELOR? OR WHO HAS FIRST GIVEN TO HIM
THAT IT MIGHT BE REPAID TO HIM? For from Him and
through Him and to Him are all things. To Him *be*
the glory forever. Amen.

ADORATION
Ps 139:17-18

How precious are Your thoughts to me, O God!
How vast is the sum of them!
If I should count them,
    they would outnumber the sand.
When I awake, I am still with You.

⤶ **Pause to adore the wisdom of God**

THANKSGIVING
Luke 15:7,
10b

I tell you that in the same way, there will be
more joy in heaven over one sinner who repents
than over ninety-nine righteous persons who
need no repentance. I tell you, there is joy in the
presence of the angels of God over one sinner
who repents.

⤶ **Pause to give thanks to God that there is hope for
the unsaved**

CONFESSION
⁺Jer 17:9-10

The heart is more deceitful than all else
And is desperately sick;
Who can know it?
You, Yahweh, search the heart;
You test the inmost being,
Even to give to each man according to his ways,
According to the fruit of his deeds.

Ps 139:23-24   Search me, O God, and know my heart;
Try me and know my anxious thoughts;
And see if there be any hurtful way in me,
And lead me in the everlasting way.

🖋 **Pause to confess to God any specific sins that are being uncovered**

AFFIRMATION   As for me, I shall call upon God,
⁺Ps 55:16-17, 22   And Yahweh will save me.
Evening and morning and at noon,
    I will bring my complaint and moan,
And He will hear my voice.
I will cast my burden upon Yahweh
    and He will sustain me;
He will never allow the righteous to be shaken.

🖋 **Pause to affirm God's truth that He hears and answers**

DISCIPLES'   Our Father who is in heaven,
PRAYER   Hallowed be Your name.
Matt 6:9b-13   Your kingdom come. Your will be done,
On earth as it is in heaven.
Give us this day our daily bread.
And forgive us our debts,
    as we also have forgiven our debtors.
And do not lead us into temptation
    but deliver us from the evil one.
For Yours is the kingdom and the power
    and the glory forever. Amen.

🕊 **Pause to delight in your Father's will in whatever way it is being shown to you**

PETITION
Ps 27:7-8

Hear, O Yahweh, when I call with my voice,
And be gracious to me and answer me.
On Your *behalf* my heart says, "Seek My face,"
"Your face, O Yahweh, I shall seek."

Ps 86:11-12

Teach me Your way, O Yahweh;
I will walk in Your truth;
Unite my heart to fear Your name.
I will give thanks to You, O Lord my God,
    with all my heart,
And will glorify Your name forever.

Ps 19:14

Let the words of my mouth
    and the meditation of my heart
Be acceptable in Your sight,
O Yahweh, my rock and my Redeemer.

🕊 **Pause to ask God about your personal needs**

INTERCESSION
⁺Matt 9:37-38

Oh Jesus, I see the crowds, and like You I feel compassion for them, because they are distressed and downcast like sheep without a shepherd. The harvest is plentiful, but the workers are few. Therefore I pray earnestly to You, the Lord of the harvest, to send out workers into Your harvest.

🖋 **Pause to intercede earnestly with God for missions and evangelistic efforts**

BENEDICTION   May Yahweh bless us, and keep us;
Num 6:24-26   May Yahweh make His face shine on us,
And be gracious to us;
May Yahweh lift up His face on us,
And give us peace.

DAY 13

ADORATION
Praise Yah! Praise God in His sanctuary;

Ps 150

Praise Him in His mighty expanse.
Praise Him for His mighty deeds;
Praise Him according to the abundance
  of His greatness.
Praise Him with trumpet blast;
Praise Him with harp and lyre.
Praise Him with tambourine and dancing;
Praise Him with stringed instruments and pipe.
Praise Him with resounding cymbals;
Praise Him with clashing cymbals.
Let everything that has breath praise Yah.
Praise Yah!

🍃 **Pause to adore God out loud!**

THANKSGIVING
But the salvation of the righteous
  is from Yahweh;

Ps 37:39-40

He is their strength in time of distress.
Yahweh helps them and protects them;
He protects them from the wicked
  and saves them,
Because they take refuge in Him.

🍃 **Pause to give thanks to God for specific blessings**

CONFESSION When I kept silent *about my sin*,
Ps 32:3-5   my bones wasted away
Through my groaning all day long.
For day and night Your hand was heavy upon me;
My vitality was drained away
    as with the heat of summer.   Selah.
I acknowledged my sin to You,
And my iniquity I did not cover up;
I said, "I will confess my transgressions
    to Yahweh;"
And You forgave the iniquity of my sin.   Selah.

Ps 139:23-24   Search me, O God, and know my heart;
Try me and know my anxious thoughts;
And see if there be any hurtful way in me,
And lead me in the everlasting way.

🖉   **Pause to confess to God any specific sins of which
you are aware**

AFFIRMATION As for me, I know that my Redeemer lives,
Job 19:25-26 And at the last He will rise up over the dust
    of this world.
Even after my skin is destroyed,
Yet from my flesh I shall behold God.

Mal 1:11   "For from the rising of the sun even to its
setting, My name *will be* great among the
nations, and in every place incense is going

to be presented to My name, as well as a grain offering *that is* clean; for My name *will be* great among the nations," says Yahweh of hosts.

᷂ **Pause to affirm that God will reign forever**

DISCIPLES' Our Father who is in heaven,
PRAYER Hallowed be Your name.
Matt 6:9b-13 Your kingdom come. Your will be done,
On earth as it is in heaven.
Give us this day our daily bread.
And forgive us our debts,
as we also have forgiven our debtors.
And do not lead us into temptation
but deliver us from the evil one.
For Yours is the kingdom and the power
and the glory forever. Amen.

᷂ **Pause to meditate on the Father's glorious power**

PETITION I pray that the God of our Lord Jesus Christ,
⁺Eph 1:17-19 the Father of glory, may give to me the Spirit of wisdom and of revelation in the full knowledge of Him, so that with the eyes of my heart having been enlightened I will know what is the hope of His calling, what are the riches of the glory of His inheritance in the saints, and what is the surpassing greatness of His power toward me according to the working of the might of His strength.

Ps 19:14   Let the words of my mouth
       and the meditation of my heart
    Be acceptable in Your sight,
    O Yahweh, my rock and my Redeemer.

🍃 **Pause to ask God about your personal needs**

INTERCESSION   Listen from heaven Your dwelling place, and
⁺2 Chr 6:30-31   forgive, and give to each person according to all
    his ways, whose heart You know, for You alone
    know the hearts of the sons of men, that they
    may fear You, to walk in Your ways all the days
    they live upon the face of the land which You
    have given to our fathers.

🍃 **Pause to intercede with God for others**

BENEDICTION   I will give thanks to You, O Lord,
Ps 57:9-11   among the peoples;
    I will sing praises to You among the nations.
    For Your lovingkindness is great to the heavens
    And Your truth to the skies.
    Be exalted above the heavens, O God;
    Let Your glory *be* above all the earth.

ADORATION
Ps 119:164-168

Seven times a day I praise You,
Because of Your righteous judgments.
Those who love Your law have much peace,
And nothing causes them to stumble.
I hope for Your salvation, O Yahweh,
And I do Your commandments.
My soul keeps Your testimonies,
And I love them exceedingly.
I keep Your precepts and Your testimonies,
For all my ways are before You.

🖎 **Pause to behold your God**

THANKSGIVING
Ps 92:1-2

It is good to give thanks to Yahweh
And to sing praises to Your name, O Most High;
To declare Your lovingkindness in the morning
And Your faithfulness by night.

🖎 **Pause to give thanks to God for specific blessings**

CONFESSION
Is 1:18

"Come now, and let us reason together,"
Says Yahweh,
"Though your sins are as scarlet,
They will be as white as snow;
Though they are red like crimson,
They will be like wool."

Ps 139:23-24 Search me, O God, and know my heart.
Try me and know my anxious thoughts;
And see if there be any hurtful way in me,
And lead me in the everlasting way.

↵ **Pause to confess to God any specific sins**

AFFIRMATION
†1 Sam 2:2, 8 I pray with Hannah:
There is no one holy like Yahweh;
Indeed, there is no one besides You,
Nor is there any rock like our God.
He raises the poor from the dust;
He exalts the needy from the ash heap
To make them sit with nobles,
And inherit a seat of glory;
For the pillars of the earth are Yahweh's,
And He set the world on them.

↵ **Pause to affirm God's truth**

DISCIPLES'   Our Father who is in heaven,
PRAYER   Hallowed be Your name.
Matt 6:9b-13 Your kingdom come. Your will be done,
On earth as it is in heaven.
Give us this day our daily bread.
And forgive us our debts,
  as we also have forgiven our debtors.
And do not lead us into temptation
  but deliver us from the evil one.

For Yours is the kingdom and the power
and the glory forever. Amen.

🍃 **Pause to reflect on how your Father's will in heaven can be realized on earth**

PETITION I bow my knees before the Father, from whom
Eph 3:14-19 every family in heaven and on earth is named,
that He would give me, according to the riches
of His glory, to be strengthened with power
through His Spirit in the inner man, that Christ
may dwell in my heart through faith; and being
firmly rooted and grounded in love, I may be
able to comprehend with all the saints what is
the breadth and length and height and depth,
and to know the love of Christ which surpasses
knowledge, that I may be filled up to all the
fullness of God.

Ps 19:14 Let the words of my mouth
and the meditation of my heart
Be acceptable in Your sight,
O Yahweh, my rock and my Redeemer.

🍃 **Pause to ask God about your personal needs**

INTERCESSION *+2 Thess* *2:16-17*	Now may our Lord Jesus Christ Himself and God our Father, who has loved us and given us eternal comfort and good hope by grace, encourage our hearts and strengthen them in every good work and word.

    ↳ **Pause to ask God to encourage those who need it**

BENEDICTION *+Jude 24-25*	Now to Him who is able to keep us from stumbling, and to make us stand in the presence of His glory blameless with great joy, to the only God our Savior, through Jesus Christ our Lord, be glory, majesty, might, and authority, before all time and now and forever. Amen.

ADORATION
Ps 103:20-22

Bless Yahweh, you His angels,
Mighty in strength, who perform His word,
Obeying the voice of His word!
Bless Yahweh, all *you* His hosts,
You who serve Him, doing His will.
Bless Yahweh, all you works of His,
In all places of His rule;
Bless Yahweh, O my soul!

↙ **Pause to adore your God**

THANKSGIVING
⁺1 Cor 15:57-58

Thanks be to God, who gives us the victory
through our Lord Jesus Christ! Therefore,
as beloved brothers, may we be steadfast,
immovable, always abounding in the work
of the Lord, knowing that our labor is not in
vain in the Lord.

↙ **Pause to give thanks to God for specific blessings**

CONFESSION
Eccl 7:20

Indeed, there is not a righteous man on earth
who *continually* does good and who never sins.

Rom 3:23

For all have sinned and fall short of the glory
of God.

Ps 139:23-24 Search me, O God, and know my heart;
Try me and know my anxious thoughts;
And see if there be any hurtful way in me,
And lead me in the everlasting way.

↵ **Pause to confess to God any specific sins that are emerging**

AFFIRMATION He keeps the feet of His holy ones,
1 Sam 2:9-10 But the wicked ones are silenced in darkness,
For not by power shall a man prevail.
Those who contend with Yahweh
    will be dismayed;
Against them He will thunder in the heavens;
Yahweh will render justice to the ends
    of the earth,
And He will give strength to His king,
And He will exalt the horn of His anointed.

↵ **Pause to affirm God's truth**

DISCIPLES' Our Father who is in heaven,
PRAYER Hallowed be Your name.
Matt 6:9b-13 Your kingdom come. Your will be done,
On earth as it is in heaven.
Give us this day our daily bread.
And forgive us our debts,
    as we also have forgiven our debtors.
And do not lead us into temptation
    but deliver us from the evil one.

For Yours is the kingdom and the power
and the glory forever. Amen.

🕊 **Pause to be grateful for Israel's daily manna and your daily food**

PETITION And this I pray, that my love may abound
Phil 1:9-11 still more and more in full knowledge and all
discernment, so that I may approve the things
that are excellent, in order to be sincere and
without fault until the day of Christ, having
been filled with the fruit of righteousness
which comes through Jesus Christ, to the
glory and praise of God.

Ps 19:14 Let the words of my mouth
and the meditation of my heart
Be acceptable in Your sight,
O Yahweh, my rock and my Redeemer.

🕊 **Pause to ask God that your love will abound**

INTERCESSION Now may our God and Father Himself and
1 Thess Jesus our Lord direct our way, and may the
3:11-13 Lord cause us to increase and abound in love
for one another, and for all people, just as we
also do for others, so that He may strengthen
our hearts blameless in holiness, before our
God and Father, at the coming of our Lord
Jesus with all His saints.

✑ **Pause to intercede with God for believers and unbelievers**

BENEDICTION
Rev 7:10b, 12b

Salvation *belongs* to our God who sits
on the throne, and to the Lamb. Amen.
The blessing and the glory and the wisdom
and the thanksgiving and the honor
and the power and the strength, *be* to our God
forever and ever. Amen.

ADORATION
Rev 5:12b-13

"Worthy is the Lamb that was slain to receive power and riches and wisdom and strength and honor and glory and blessing." And every created thing which is in heaven and on the earth and under the earth and on the sea, and all things in them, I heard saying, "To Him who sits on the throne, and to the Lamb, *be* the blessing and the honor and the glory and the might forever and ever."

⤙ **Pause to worship the Lamb**

THANKSGIVING
⁺1 Thess 5:16-18

I will rejoice always; I will pray without ceasing; in everything I will give thanks, for this is God's will for me in Christ Jesus.

⤙ **Pause to give thanks to God for both the good and the bad things you face**

CONFESSION
Ps 25:8-11; 16-18

Good and upright is Yahweh;
Therefore He instructs sinners in the way.
May He lead the humble in justice,
And may He teach the humble His way.
All the paths of Yahweh are lovingkindness
    and truth
To those who guard His covenant

and His testimonies.
For Your name's sake, O Yahweh,
Pardon my iniquity, for it is great.
Turn to me and be gracious to me,
For I am alone and afflicted.
The troubles of my heart are enlarged;
Bring me out of my distresses.
See my affliction and my trouble,
And forgive all my sins.

Ps 139:23-24 Search me, O God, and know my heart;
Try me and know my anxious thoughts;
And see if there be any hurtful way in me,
And lead me in the everlasting way.

✍ **Pause to confess to God any specific sins that come to mind**

AFFIRMATION The God who made the world and all things in
Acts 17:24-28a it, since He is Lord of heaven and earth, does not
dwell in temples made with hands; nor is He
served by human hands, as though He needed
anything, since He Himself gives to all *people*
life and breath and all things; and He made from
one *man* every nation of mankind to inhabit all
the face of the earth, having determined *their*
appointed times and the boundaries of their
habitation, that they would seek God, if perhaps
they might grope for Him and find Him, though
He is not far from each one of us; for in Him we
live and move and exist.

> 🍃 Pause to affirm God's creation and His common grace to all

<table>
<tr><td>DISCIPLES'
PRAYER
Matt 6:9b-13</td><td>Our Father who is in heaven,
Hallowed be Your name.
Your kingdom come. Your will be done,
   On earth as it is in heaven.
Give us this day our daily bread.
And forgive us our debts,
     as we also have forgiven our debtors.
And do not lead us into temptation
     but deliver us from the evil one.
For Yours is the kingdom and the power
     and the glory forever. Amen.</td></tr>
</table>

> 🍃 Pause to decide how you can show to others the Father's mercy shown to you

PETITION
James 5:16b-18

The effective prayer of a righteous man can accomplish much. Elijah was a man with a nature like ours, and he prayed earnestly that it would not rain, and it did not rain on the earth for three years and six months. Then he prayed again, and the sky gave rain and the earth produced its fruit.

Ps 19:14

Let the words of my mouth
   and the meditation of my heart
Be acceptable in Your sight,
O Yahweh, my rock and my Redeemer.

Pause to ask God to grant His mercy to you so you can show mercy to others

---

INTERCESSION
Ps 44:4-8

You are my King, O God;
Command salvation for Jacob.
Through You we will push back our adversaries;
Through Your name we will tread down
 those who rise up against us.
For I will not trust in my bow,
And my sword will not save me.
But You have saved us from our adversaries,
And You have put to shame those who hate us.
In God we have boasted all day long,
And we will give thanks to Your name forever.
          Selah.

⁺Matt 5:44-45

Lord, show me how to balance these following requests. I desire to love my enemies and pray for those who persecute me, so that I may be a son of my Father who is in heaven; for He causes His sun to rise on the evil and the good and sends rain on the righteous and the unrighteous.

Pause to intercede with God for those who oppose your testimony

---

BENEDICTION
⁺2 Cor 13:14

The grace of the Lord Jesus Christ, and the love of God, and the fellowship of the Holy Spirit, be with us all.

DAY 17

ADORATION
Ps 34:1-3

I will bless Yahweh at all times;
His praise shall continually be in my mouth.
My soul will make its boast in Yahweh;
The humble will hear it and rejoice.
O magnify Yahweh with me,
And let us exalt His name together.

🍃 **Pause to adore God with someone else today**

THANKSGIVING
⁺Eph 2:19-22

Lord, I thank you that I am no longer a stranger
and sojourner, but I am a fellow citizen with
the saints, and I am of God's household, having
been built on the foundation of the apostles and
prophets, Christ Jesus Himself being the corner
stone, in whom the whole building, being joined
together, is growing into a holy sanctuary in the
Lord, in whom I also am being built together
into a dwelling of God in the Spirit.

🍃 **Pause to give thanks to God for being part of His family**

CONFESSION
Is 1:18

"Come now, and let us reason together,"
Says Yahweh,
"Though your sins are as scarlet,
They will be as white as snow;
Though they are red like crimson,
They will be like wool."

Ps 139:23-24   Search me, O God, and know my heart;
Try me and know my anxious thoughts;
And see if there be any hurtful way in me,
And lead me in the everlasting way.

↙ **Pause to confess to God any wrong thoughts**

AFFIRMATION   With the Lord one day is like a thousand
⁺*2 Pet 3:8b-9*   years, and a thousand years like one day.
The Lord is not slow about His promise,
as some consider slowness, but is patient
toward us, not willing for any to perish but
for all to come to repentance.

↙ **Pause to affirm the hope of the Second Coming**

DISCIPLES'   Our Father who is in heaven,
PRAYER   Hallowed be Your name.
Matt 6:9b-13   Your kingdom come. Your will be done,
On earth as it is in heaven.
Give us this day our daily bread.
And forgive us our debts,
    as we also have forgiven our debtors.
And do not lead us into temptation
    but deliver us from the evil one.
For Yours is the kingdom and the power
    and the glory forever. Amen.

↲ **Pause to pray for your spiritual armor so you can resist the devil's schemes**

PETITION
Ps 121:1-3
I will lift up my eyes to the mountains;
From where shall my help come?
My help comes from Yahweh,
Who made heaven and earth.
He will not allow your foot to stumble;
He who keeps you will not slumber.

Ps 19:14
Let the words of my mouth
    and the meditation of my heart
Be acceptable in Your sight,
O Yahweh, my rock and my Redeemer.

↲ **Pause to ask God for His help in your daily tasks**

INTERCESSION
†Rom 8:26-27
And in the same way the Spirit also helps our weakness, for I do not know how to pray as I should, but the Spirit Himself intercedes for me with groanings too deep for words; and He who searches the hearts knows what the mind of the Spirit is, because He intercedes for the saints according to the will of God.

↲ **Pause to ask God what you should pray for**

Now to Him who is able to strengthen me according to the gospel and the preaching of Jesus Christ, according to the revelation of the mystery which has been kept secret for long ages past, but now is manifested, and by the Scriptures of the prophets, according to the commandment of the eternal God, has been made known to all the Gentiles, leading to obedience of faith; to the only wise God, through Jesus Christ, be the glory forever. Amen.

DAY 18

ADORATION
Ps 5:1-3
Give ear to my words, O Yahweh,
Consider my meditation.
Give heed to the sound of my cry for help,
    my King and my God,
For to You I pray.
O Yahweh, in the morning,
    You will hear my voice;
In the morning I will order *my prayer* to You
    and *eagerly* watch.

🖐 **Pause to worship your God morning, noon, and night**

THANKSGIVING
⁺Col 2:6-7
Therefore as I received Christ Jesus the Lord,
I pray that I will walk in Him, having been
firmly rooted and being built up in Him, and
having been established in my faith—just
as I was instructed—and abounding with
thanksgiving.

🖐 **Pause to thank God that you WILL bear fruit today**

CONFESSION
Ps 51:1-3
Be gracious to me, O God,
    according to Your lovingkindness;
According to the abundance of Your
    compassion blot out my transgressions.
Wash me thoroughly from my iniquity

And cleanse me from my sin.
For I know my transgressions,
And my sin is ever before me.

Ps 139:23-24 Search me, O God, and know my heart;
Try me and know my anxious thoughts;
And see if there be any hurtful way in me,
And lead me in the everlasting way.

🖋 **Pause to confess your sins to God, both thoughts and deeds**

AFFIRMATION In my distress I called upon Yahweh,
Ps 18:6 And cried to my God for help;
He heard my voice out of His temple,
And my cry for help before Him
came into His ears.

Ps 34:18-20 Yahweh is near to the brokenhearted
And saves those who are crushed in spirit.
Many are the evils *against* the righteous,
But Yahweh delivers him out of them all.
He keeps all his bones,
Not one of them is broken.

🖋 **Pause to thank God for His mercy in delivering us from so many things**

DISCIPLES' Our Father who is in heaven,
PRAYER Hallowed be Your name.
Matt 6:9b-13 Your kingdom come. Your will be done,

On earth as it is in heaven.
Give us this day our daily bread.
And forgive us our debts,
as we also have forgiven our debtors.
And do not lead us into temptation
but deliver us from the evil one.
For Yours is the kingdom and the power
and the glory forever. Amen.

🍃 **Pause to meditate on the glorious power of the Father's kingdom**

PETITION

Ps 143:7-9

Answer me quickly, O Yahweh,
my spirit wastes away;
Do not hide Your face from me,
Or I will become like those who go down
to the pit.
Cause me to hear Your lovingkindness
in the morning;
For I trust in You;
Cause me to know the way in which I
should walk;
For to You I lift up my soul.
Deliver me from my enemies, O Yahweh,
I have concealed *myself* in You.

Ps 19:14

Let the words of my mouth
and the meditation of my heart
Be acceptable in Your sight,
O Yahweh, my rock and my Redeemer.

> ⤳ **Pause to ask God to keep you safe from those who may want to hurt you**

INTERCESSION
Ps 124

"Had it not been Yahweh who was on our side,"
Let Israel now say,
"Had it not been Yahweh who was on our side
When men rose up against us,
Then they would have swallowed us alive,
When their anger was kindled against us;
Then the waters would have flowed over us,
The stream would have swept over our soul;
Then the raging waters would have swept
over our soul."
Blessed be Yahweh,
Who has not given us to be prey for their teeth.
Our soul has escaped as a bird out of the snare
of the trapper;
The snare is broken and we have escaped.
Our help is in the name of Yahweh,
Who made heaven and earth.

> ⤳ **Pause to intercede for others who are facing serious physical or spiritual difficulties**

BENEDICTION
⁺Num 6:24-26

May Yahweh bless us, and keep us;
May Yahweh make His face shine on us,
And be gracious to us;
May Yahweh lift up His face on us,
And give us peace.

ADORATION
Ps 119:164-168

Seven times a day I praise You,
Because of Your righteous judgments.
Those who love Your law have much peace,
And nothing causes them to stumble.
I hope for Your salvation, O Yahweh,
And I do Your commandments.
My soul keeps Your testimonies,
And I love them exceedingly.
I keep Your precepts and Your testimonies,
For all my ways are before You.

⮌ **Pause to adore your God over and over**

THANKSGIVING
Ps 100

Make a loud shout to Yahweh, all the earth.
Serve Yahweh with gladness;
Come before Him with joyful songs.
Know that Yahweh, He is God;
It is He who has made us, and not we ourselves;
We are His people and the sheep of His pasture.
Enter His gates with thanksgiving
And His courts with praise.
Give thanks to Him, bless His name.
For Yahweh is good;
His lovingkindness endures forever
And His faithfulness, generation
    unto generation.

🕊 **Pause to give thanks to God for His faithfulness even when we are unfaithful**

CONFESSION
2 Tim 2:19

Nevertheless, the firm foundation of God stands, having this seal, "THE LORD KNOWS THOSE WHO ARE HIS," and, "EVERYONE WHO NAMES THE NAME OF THE LORD IS TO DEPART FROM WICKEDNESS."

Ps 139:23-24

Search me, O God, and know my heart;
Try me and know my anxious thoughts;
And see if there be any hurtful way in me,
And lead me in the everlasting way.

🕊 **Pause to confess to God any hurtful ideas that you may have**

AFFIRMATION
Ps 10:17-18

O Yahweh, You have heard the desire
    of the humble;
You will strengthen their heart, You will cause
    Your ear to give heed
To give justice to the orphan and the oppressed,
So that man who is of the earth will no longer
    cause terror.

🕊 **Pause to affirm that God loves the oppressed and ask Him to help you do so too**

DISCIPLES'
PRAYER
Matt 6:9b-13

Our Father who is in heaven,
Hallowed be Your name.
Your kingdom come. Your will be done,
On earth as it is in heaven.

Give us this day our daily bread.
And forgive us our debts,
    as we also have forgiven our debtors.
And do not lead us into temptation
    but deliver us from the evil one.
For Yours is the kingdom and the power
    and the glory forever. Amen.

Pause to recognize that although God is in heaven He can still be addressed as your Father

PETITION
Ps 27:4

One thing I have asked from Yahweh,
    that I shall seek:
That I may dwell in the house of Yahweh
    all the days of my life,
To behold the beauty of Yahweh
And to inquire in His temple.

Ps 86:11-12

Teach me Your way, O Yahweh;
I will walk in Your truth;
Unite my heart to fear Your name.
I will give thanks to You, O Lord my God,
    with all my heart,
And will glorify Your name forever.

Ps 19:14

Let the words of my mouth
    and the meditation of my heart
Be acceptable in Your sight,
O Yahweh, my rock and my Redeemer.

⤺ **Pause to simply gaze at God for a few moments**

INTERCESSION
James 5:13-15

Is anyone among you suffering? Then he must pray. Is anyone cheerful? He is to sing praises. Is anyone among you sick? Then he must call for the elders of the church and they are to pray over him, anointing him with oil in the name of the Lord. And the prayer offered in faith will save the one who is sick, and the Lord will raise him up, and if he has committed sins, they will be forgiven him. Lord, I intercede for the sick and the suffering and the sinful.

⤺ **Pause to intercede with God for sufferers, physically and spiritually**

BENEDICTION
Eph 3:20-21

Now to Him who is able to do far more abundantly beyond all that we ask or understand, according to the power that works within us, to Him *be* the glory in the church and in Christ Jesus to all generations forever and ever. Amen.

ADORATION Praise Yah!

Ps 148:1-5 Praise Yahweh from the heavens;
Praise Him in the heights!
Praise Him, all His angels;
Praise Him, all His hosts!
Praise Him, sun and moon;
Praise Him, all stars of light!
Praise Him, heavens of heavens,
And the waters that are above the heavens!
Let them praise the name of Yahweh,
For He commanded and they were created.

Pause to adore God for all of His creation

THANKSGIVING Praise Yah!

Ps 111:1-6 I will give thanks to Yahweh with all *my* heart,
In the council of the upright
and in the congregation.
Great are the works of Yahweh;
They are sought by all who delight in them.
Splendid and majestic is His work,
And His righteousness stands forever.
He has made His wondrous deeds
to be remembered;
Yahweh is gracious and compassionate.
He has given food to those who fear Him;

He will remember His covenant forever.
He has declared to His people the power
of His works,
In giving them an inheritance of the nations.

✍ **Pause to thank God for so many things you take for granted**

CONFESSION
2 Chr 7:13-14
If I shut up the heavens so that there is no rain,
or if I command the grasshopper to devour
the land, or if I send pestilence among My people,
and My people who are called by My name
humble themselves and pray and seek My face
and turn from their evil ways, then I will listen
from heaven, I will forgive their sin, and I will
heal their land.

Ps 139:23-24
Search me, O God, and know my heart;
Try me and know my anxious thoughts;
And see if there be any hurtful way in me,
And lead me in the everlasting way.

✍ **Pause to confess to God both known and unknown sins**

AFFIRMATION
Hab 2:4
Behold, as for the proud one,
His soul is not right within him;
But the righteous will live by his faith.

✍ **Pause to pray that the proud will be humbled in God's way**

Our Father who is in heaven,
Hallowed be Your name.
Your kingdom come. Your will be done,
On earth as it is in heaven.
Give us this day our daily bread.
And forgive us our debts,
as we also have forgiven our debtors.
And do not lead us into temptation
but deliver us from the evil one.
For Yours is the kingdom and the power
and the glory forever. Amen.

✍ **Pause to recognize that your Father's "name" is more than a title but embodies all that He is**

PETITION I am praying at all times with all prayer and
Eph 6:18-20 petition in the Spirit, and to this end, being
on the alert with all perseverance and petition
for all the saints, as well as on my behalf, that
words may be given to me in the opening of
my mouth, to make known with boldness
the mystery of the gospel—for which I am
an ambassador—so that in proclaiming it
I may speak boldly, as I ought to speak.

Ps 19:14 Let the words of my mouth
and the meditation of my heart
Be acceptable in Your sight,
O Yahweh, my rock and my Redeemer.

🖎 Pause to ask God to help you be bold in your witness

INTERCESSION *Ps 44:4-8*	You are my King, O God; Command salvation for Jacob. Through You we will push back our adversaries; Through Your name we will tread down 　　those who rise up against us. For I will not trust in my bow, And my sword will not save me. But You have saved us from our adversaries, And You have put to shame those who hate us. In God we have boasted all day long, And we will give thanks to Your name forever. 　　　　　　　　　　　　　　　　Selah.

🖎 Pause to intercede with God for those neighbors or co-workers who anger you

BENEDICTION *Ps 135:5-6*	For I know that Yahweh is great And that our Lord is *greater* than all gods. Whatever Yahweh pleases, He does, In heaven and on earth, in the seas 　　and in all deeps.
Ps 135:13	O Yahweh, Your name is everlasting, O Yahweh, Your remembrance 　　is from generation to generation.

ADORATION
⁺Heb 1:3-4

I exalt Him whom the Father appointed heir of all things, through whom also He made the worlds, who is the radiance of the Father's glory and the exact representation of His nature, and who upholds all things by the word of His power; who, having accomplished cleansing for sins, sat down at the right hand of the Majesty on high, having become so much better than the angels, as He has inherited a more excellent name than they.

↰ **Pause to adore and to glorify and to magnify your Savior**

THANKSGIVING
2 Cor 5:9-10

Therefore we also have as our ambition, whether at home or absent, to be pleasing to Him. For we must all appear before the judgment seat of Christ, so that each one may be recompensed for his deeds in the body, according to what he has done, whether good or bad.

↰ **Pause to give thanks to God that he knows all things about you**

CONFESSION
James 5:16

Therefore, confess your sins to one another, and pray for one another so that you may be healed. The effective prayer of a righteous man can accomplish much.

Ps 139:23-24   Search me, O God, and know my heart;
Try me and know my anxious thoughts;
And see if there be any hurtful way in me,
And lead me in the everlasting way.

↙ **Pause to confess to God that thing that you know you are doing that is wrong**

AFFIRMATION   Yahweh is near to the brokenhearted
Ps 34:18-20   And saves those who are crushed in spirit.
Many are the evils *against* the righteous,
But Yahweh delivers him out of them all.
He keeps all his bones,
Not one of them is broken.

↙ **Pause to affirm that God really cares for the hurting**

DISCIPLES'   Our Father who is in heaven,
PRAYER   Hallowed be Your name.
Matt 6:9b-13   Your kingdom come. Your will be done,
On earth as it is in heaven.
Give us this day our daily bread.
And forgive us our debts,
      as we also have forgiven our debtors.
And do not lead us into temptation
      but deliver us from the evil one.
For Yours is the kingdom and the power
      and the glory forever. Amen.

≤ **Pause to recognize how God's kingdom is both now and also yet to come**

PETITION   I will lift up my eyes to the mountains;
Ps 121   From where shall my help come?
My help *comes* from Yahweh,
Who made heaven and earth.
He will not allow your foot to stumble;
He who keeps you will not slumber.
Behold, He who keeps Israel
Will not slumber and will not sleep.
Yahweh is your keeper;
Yahweh is your shade on your right hand.
The sun will not strike you by day,
Nor the moon by night.
Yahweh will keep you from all evil;
He will keep your soul.
Yahweh will keep your going out
    and your coming in
From now until forever.

Ps 19:14   Let the words of my mouth
    and the meditation of my heart
Be acceptable in Your sight,
O Yahweh, my rock and my Redeemer.

≤ **Pause to ask God about safety in your driving and travels**

INTERCESSION

⁺Jude 20-23

May we, beloved, build ourselves up on our most holy faith, and praying in the Holy Spirit, may You keep us in the love of God, waiting for the mercy of our Lord Jesus Christ to eternal life. And on some, who are doubting, may we have mercy; and I pray for others, Lord, that You save them by snatching them out of the fire; and on others may You show mercy with fear, as we hate even the tunic polluted by the flesh.

٭ Pause to intercede for doubters and others in danger of backsliding

BENEDICTION

⁺Rom 16:25-27

Now to Him who is able to strengthen us according to the gospel and the preaching of Jesus Christ, according to the revelation of the mystery which has been kept secret for long ages past, but now is manifested, and by the Scriptures of the prophets, according to the commandment of the eternal God, has been made known to all the Gentiles, leading to obedience of faith; to the only wise God, through Jesus Christ, be the glory forever. Amen.

ADORATION
Ps 42:1-2

As the deer pants for the water brooks,
So my soul pants for You, O God.
My soul thirsts for God, for the living God;
When shall I come and appear before God?

⁺*Ps 94:22*

Yahweh, You are my stronghold,
And my God the rock of my refuge.

✑ **Pause to adore your God over and over**

THANKSGIVING
⁺*1 Cor 15:57-58*

Thanks be to God, who gives us the victory
through our Lord Jesus Christ! Therefore,
my beloved brothers, may we be steadfast,
immovable, always abounding in the work
of the Lord, knowing that our labor is not in
vain in the Lord.

✑ **Pause to thank God for victories experienced**

CONFESSION
Eccl 7:20

Indeed, there is not a righteous man on earth
who *continually* does good and who never sins.

Ps 139:23-24

Search me, O God, and know my heart;
Try me and know my anxious thoughts;
And see if there be any hurtful way in me,
And lead me in the everlasting way.

↙ **Pause to confess to God any secret sins**

AFFIRMATION

Ps 1:1-3 How blessed is the man who does not walk
    in the counsel of the wicked,
Nor stand in the way of sinners,
Nor sit in the seat of scoffers!
But his delight is in the law of Yahweh,
And in His law he meditates day and night.
And he will be like a tree *firmly* planted
    by streams of water,
Which yields its fruit in its season
And its leaf does not wither;
And in whatever he does, he prospers.

Ps 119:97 Oh how I love Your law!
It is my meditation all the day.

↙ **Pause to affirm God's law and meditate in it for a while**

DISCIPLES'
PRAYER
Matt 6:9b-13 Our Father who is in heaven,
Hallowed be Your name.
Your kingdom come. Your will be done,
On earth as it is in heaven.
Give us this day our daily bread.
And forgive us our debts,
    as we also have forgiven our debtors.
And do not lead us into temptation
    but deliver us from the evil one.
For Yours is the kingdom and the power
    and the glory forever. Amen.

𝄬 **Pause to delight in your Father's will in whatever way it is being shown to you**

PETITION
⁺John 15:7-11 If I abide in Him, and His words abide in me, I can ask whatever I wish, and it will be done for me. My Father is glorified by this, that I bear much fruit, and so prove to be His disciple. Just as the Father has loved the Son, He has also loved me; so I am to abide in His love. If I keep His commandments, I will abide in His love; just as He kept His Father's commandments and abides in His love. Jesus spoke these things so that His joy may be in me, and that my joy may be complete.

Ps 19:14 Let the words of my mouth
and the meditation of my heart
Be acceptable in Your sight,
O Yahweh, my rock and my Redeemer.

𝄬 **Pause to ask God to nurture your own fruit-bearing**

INTERCESSION
Ps 44:4-8 You are my King, O God;
Command salvation for Jacob.
Through You we will push back our adversaries;
Through Your name we will tread down
those who rise up against us.
For I will not trust in my bow,
And my sword will not save me.
But You have saved us from our adversaries,

And You have put to shame those who hate us.
In God we have boasted all day long,
And we will give thanks to Your name forever.

Selah.

Matt 5:44-45 I also desire to love my enemies and pray for
those who persecute me, so that I may be a son
of my Father who is in heaven; for He causes
His sun to rise on the evil and the good, and
sends rain on the righteous and the unrighteous.

ↆ **Pause to intercede with God for those people you do not like**

BENEDICTION Now to Him who is able to do far more abundantly
Eph 3:20-21 beyond all that we ask or understand, according to
the power that works within us, to Him *be* the glory
in the church and in Christ Jesus to all generations
forever and ever. Amen.

ADORATION
Ps 8:1-4

O Yahweh, our Lord,
How majestic is Your name in all the earth,
Who displays Your splendor
    above the heavens!
From the mouth of infants and nursing babies
    You have established strength
Because of Your adversaries,
To make the enemy and the revengeful cease.
When I see Your heavens,
    the work of Your fingers,
The moon and the stars,
    which You have established;
What is man that You remember him,
And the son of man that You care for him?

🌿 **Pause to magnify God's creation**

THANKSGIVING
Ps 5:11-12

But let all who take refuge in You be glad,
Let them ever sing for joy;
And may You shelter them,
That those who love Your name
    may exult in You.
For it is You who blesses the righteous one,
    O Yahweh,
You surround him with favor
    as with a large shield.

✍ **Pause to give thanks to God for protection from dangers**

CONFESSION
Ps 25:6-11

Remember, O Yahweh, Your compassion
   and Your lovingkindnesses,
For they have been from of old.
Do not remember the sins of my youth
   or my transgressions;
According to Your lovingkindness remember me,
For the sake of Your goodness, O Yahweh.
Good and upright is Yahweh;
Therefore He instructs sinners in the way.
May He lead the humble in justice,
And may He teach the humble His way.
All the paths of Yahweh are lovingkindness
   and truth
To those who guard His covenant
   and His testimonies.
For Your name's sake, O Yahweh,
Pardon my iniquity, for it is great.

Ps 139:23-24

Search me, O God, and know my heart;
Try me and know my anxious thoughts;
And see if there be any hurtful way in me,
And lead me in the everlasting way.

✍ **Pause to ask God's forgiveness for those sins that sometimes dominate you**

He keeps the feet of His holy ones,
But the wicked ones are silenced in darkness,
For not by power shall a man prevail.
Those who contend with Yahweh
   will be dismayed;
Against them He will thunder in the heavens;
Yahweh will render justice to the ends
   of the earth,
And He will give strength to His king,
And He will exalt the horn of His anointed.

📖 **Pause to thank God for His protection that we often take for granted**

Our Father who is in heaven,
Hallowed be Your name.
Your kingdom come. Your will be done,
On earth as it is in heaven.
Give us this day our daily bread.
And forgive us our debts,
   as we also have forgiven our debtors.
And do not lead us into temptation
   but deliver us from the evil one.
For Yours is the kingdom and the power
   and the glory forever. Amen.

📖 **Pause to reflect on how your Father's will in heaven can be realized on earth**

PETITION
James
5:16b-18

The effective prayer of a righteous man can accomplish much. Elijah was a man with a nature like ours, and he prayed earnestly that it would not rain, and it did not rain on the earth for three years and six months. Then he prayed again, and the sky gave rain and the earth produced its fruit.

Ps 19:14

Let the words of my mouth
    and the meditation of my heart
Be acceptable in Your sight,
O Yahweh, my rock and my Redeemer.

↙ **Pause to ask God to do what is humanly impossible for someone**

INTERCESSION
†James
5:19-20

My brothers, if any among you strays from the truth and one turns him back, let him know that he who turns a sinner from the error of his way will save his soul from death and will cover a multitude of sins. Lord, bring back those of my family and friends who have strayed from You.

↙ **Pause to intercede with God for those who have strayed from Him**

BENEDICTION
†2 Cor 13:14

The grace of the Lord Jesus Christ, and the love of God, and the fellowship of the Holy Spirit, be with us all.

ADORATION
Rev 7:9-12

After these things I looked, and behold, a great multitude which no one could count, from every nation and *all* tribes and peoples and tongues, standing before the throne and before the Lamb, clothed in white robes, and palm branches *were* in their hands; and they cry out with a loud voice, saying, "Salvation *belongs* to our God who sits on the throne, and to the Lamb." And all the angels were standing around the throne and the elders and the four living creatures, and they fell on their faces before the throne and worshiped God, saying, "Amen, the blessing and the glory and the wisdom and the thanksgiving and the honor and the power and the strength, *be* to our God forever and ever. Amen."

🍃 **Pause to worship the Lamb**

THANKSGIVING
⁺*Ps 107:8-9*

Let us give thanks to Yahweh
for His lovingkindness,
And for His wondrous deeds to the sons of men!
For He has satisfied the thirsty soul,
And the hungry soul He has filled
with what is good.

🍃 **Pause to give thanks to God for natural blessings like life and health and even the weather**

CONFESSION
1 John 1:8-9

If we say that we have no sin, we deceive ourselves and the truth is not in us. If we confess our sins, He is faithful and righteous to forgive us our sins and to cleanse us from all unrighteousness.

Ps 139:23-24

Search me, O God, and know my heart;
Try me and know my anxious thoughts;
And see if there be any hurtful way in me,
And lead me in the everlasting way.

🍃 **Pause to confess to God any secret sins**

AFFIRMATION
Ps 18:30-32

As for God, His way is blameless;
The word of Yahweh is tried;
He is a shield to all who take refuge in Him.
For who is God, but Yahweh?
And who is a rock, except our God,
The God who girds me with strength
And makes my way blameless?

John 4:23-24

But an hour is coming, and now is, when the true worshipers will worship the Father in spirit and truth; for such people the Father seeks to be His worshipers. God is spirit, and those who worship Him must worship in spirit and truth.

🍃 **Pause to affirm God's unchangeable character**

DISCIPLES'
PRAYER
Matt 6:9b-13

Our Father who is in heaven,
Hallowed be Your name.
Your kingdom come. Your will be done,
On earth as it is in heaven.
Give us this day our daily bread.
And forgive us our debts,
    as we also have forgiven our debtors.
And do not lead us into temptation
    but deliver us from the evil one.
For Yours is the kingdom and the power
    and the glory forever. Amen.

ᘐ **Pause to be grateful for Israel's daily manna and your daily food**

PETITION
⁺Phil 1:9-11

And this I pray, that my love may abound still more and more in full knowledge and all discernment, so that I may approve the things that are excellent, in order to be sincere and without fault until the day of Christ, having been filled with the fruit of righteousness which comes through Jesus Christ, to the glory and praise of God.

Ps 19:14

Let the words of my mouth
    and the meditation of my heart
Be acceptable in Your sight,
O Yahweh, my rock and my Redeemer.

ᘐ **Pause to ask God about your personal needs**

Yahweh is my light and my salvation;
Whom shall I fear?
Yahweh is the strong defense of my life;
Whom shall I dread?
When evildoers came upon me
    to devour my flesh,
My adversaries and my enemies,
    they stumbled and fell.
Though a host encamp against me,
My heart will not fear;
Though war arise against me,
In this I trust.
One thing I have asked from Yahweh,
    that I shall seek:
That I may dwell in the house of Yahweh
    all the days of my life,
To behold the beauty of Yahweh
And to inquire in His temple.

🦻 **Pause to intercede with God again for opponents and troublemakers**

May Yahweh bless us, and keep us;
May Yahweh make His face shine on us,
And be gracious to us;
May Yahweh lift up His face on us,
And give us peace.

ADORATION
Ps 121:1-4

I will lift up my eyes to the mountains;
From where shall my help come?
My help *comes* from Yahweh,
Who made heaven and earth.
He will not allow my foot to stumble;
He who keeps me will not slumber.
Behold, He who keeps Israel
Will not slumber and will not sleep.

> Pause to adore your God for His creation and power

THANKSGIVING
Ps 92:1-2

It is good to give thanks to Yahweh
And to sing praises to Your name, O Most High;
To declare Your lovingkindness in the morning
And Your faithfulness by night.

> Pause to give thanks to God for His lovingkindness and
> His faithfulness

CONFESSION
Ps 19:12-13

Who can discern *his* errors?
   Acquit me of hidden *faults.*
Also keep back Your slave
   from presumptuous *sins*;
Let them not rule over me;
Then I will be blameless,
And I shall be acquitted of great transgression.

Ps 139:23-24 Search me, O God, and know my heart;
Try me and know my anxious thoughts;
And see if there be any hurtful way in me,
And lead me in the everlasting way.

🍂 **Pause to confess to God both hidden and willful sins**

AFFIRMATION There is no one holy like Yahweh;
1 Sam 2:2 Indeed, there is no one besides You,
Nor is there any rock like our God.

Is 57:15 For thus says the One high and lifted up
Who dwells forever, whose name is Holy,
"I dwell *on* a high and holy place,
And *also* with the crushed and lowly of spirit
In order to revive the spirit of the lowly
And to revive the heart of the crushed."

🍂 **Pause to thank Him that in Jesus He is both high and holy and meek and lowly**

DISCIPLES' Our Father who is in heaven,
PRAYER Hallowed be Your name.
Matt 6:9b-13 Your kingdom come. Your will be done,
On earth as it is in heaven.
Give us this day our daily bread.
And forgive us our debts,
    as we also have forgiven our debtors.
And do not lead us into temptation
    but deliver us from the evil one.

For Yours is the kingdom and the power
and the glory forever. Amen.

🍃 **Pause to decide how you can show to others the Father's mercy shown to you**

PETITION
†1 Pet 3:8-9
May I and my fellow believers be like-minded,
sympathetic, brotherly, tender-hearted, and
humble in spirit; not returning evil for evil
or reviling for reviling, but giving a blessing
instead, for we were called for the very purpose
that we might inherit a blessing.

†2 Thess 3:5
May the Lord direct my heart into the love of
God and into the steadfastness of Christ.

Ps 19:14
Let the words of my mouth
and the meditation of my heart
Be acceptable in Your sight,
O Yahweh, my rock and my Redeemer.

🍃 **Pause to ask God to make you understanding of others**

INTERCESSION
Ps 3:8
Salvation belongs to Yahweh;
Your blessing *be* upon Your people!   Selah.

†Heb 13:16
May I not neglect doing good and sharing,
for with such sacrifices God is pleased.

🍃 **Pause to intercede with God for the needy**

BENEDICTION

†Jude 24-25

Now to Him who is able to keep us from stumbling, and to make us stand in the presence of His glory blameless with great joy, to the only God our Savior, through Jesus Christ our Lord, be glory, majesty, might, and authority, before all time and now and forever. Amen.

ADORATION Praise Yah!

Ps 148:1-5 Praise Yahweh from the heavens;
Praise Him in the heights!
Praise Him, all His angels;
Praise Him, all His hosts!
Praise Him, sun and moon;
Praise Him, all stars of light!
Praise Him, heavens of heavens,
And the waters that are above the heavens!
Let them praise the name of Yahweh,
For He commanded and they were created.

↙ **Pause to join the heavenly host in adoring your God**

THANKSGIVING This poor man called out,

Ps 34:6-7   and Yahweh heard him
And saved him out of all his troubles.
The angel of Yahweh encamps
    around those who fear Him,
And rescues them.

↙ **Pause to give thanks to God for His protection**

CONFESSION
Jon 4:2b

I know that You are a gracious and compassionate God, slow to anger and abundant in lovingkindness, and one who relents concerning evil.

Ps 139:23-24

Search me, O God, and know my heart;
Try me and know my anxious thoughts;
And see if there be any hurtful way in me,
And lead me in the everlasting way.

↙ **Pause to confess and thank God for not punishing you when you deserve it**

AFFIRMATION
Job 19:25-26

As for me, I know that my Redeemer lives,
And at the last He will rise up over the dust
        of this world.
Even after my skin is destroyed,
Yet from my flesh I shall behold God.

⁺Mal 1:11

For from the rising of the sun even to its setting, Your name will be great among the nations, and in every place incense is going to be presented to Your name, as well as a grain offering that is clean; for Your name will be great among the nations, O Yahweh of hosts.

↙ **Pause to affirm that God will reign visibly one day**

Our Father who is in heaven,
Hallowed be Your name.
Your kingdom come. Your will be done,
On earth as it is in heaven.
Give us this day our daily bread.
And forgive us our debts,
    as we also have forgiven our debtors.
And do not lead us into temptation
    but deliver us from the evil one.
For Yours is the kingdom and the power
    and the glory forever. Amen.

✒ **Pause to pray for your spiritual armor so you can resist the devil's schemes**

PETITION
Ps 27:7-8
Hear, O Yahweh, when I call with my voice,
And be gracious to me and answer me.
On Your *behalf* my heart says, "Seek My face,"
"Your face, O Yahweh, I shall seek."

Ps 19:14
Let the words of my mouth
    and the meditation of my heart
Be acceptable in Your sight,
O Yahweh, my rock and my Redeemer.

✒ **Pause to ask God to be patient when you are not**

INTERCESSION
*1 Thess
3:11-13
Now may our God and Father Himself and Jesus our Lord direct our way, and may the Lord cause us to increase and abound in love for one another, and for all people, just as we also do, so that He may strengthen our hearts blameless in holiness, before our God and Father, at the coming of our Lord Jesus with all His saints.

🖐 **Pause to intercede with God to increase your love for others**

BENEDICTION
*Num 6:24-26
Yahweh bless us, and keep us;
Yahweh make His face shine on us,
And be gracious to us;
Yahweh lift up His face on us,
And give us peace.

ADORATION

Ps 36:5-9

Your lovingkindness, O Yahweh,
   is in the heavens,
Your faithfulness *reaches* to the skies.
Your righteousness is like the mountains of God;
Your judgments are *like* a great deep.
O Yahweh, You save man and beast.
How precious is Your lovingkindness, O God!
And the sons of men take refuge in the shadow
   of Your wings.
They are satisfied from the richness
   of Your house;
And You give them to drink of the river
   of Your delights.
For with You is the fountain of life;
In Your light we see light.

⮒ **Pause to adore your God for His righteous judgments**

THANKSGIVING

Luke 15:7, 10b

I tell you that in the same way, there will be
more joy in heaven over one sinner who repents
than over ninety-nine righteous persons who
need no repentance. I tell you, there is joy in the
presence of the angels of God over one sinner
who repents.

⮒ **Pause to give thanks to God for His mercy toward us
sinners**

Remember, O Yahweh, Your compassion
  and Your lovingkindnesses,
For they have been from of old.
Do not remember the sins of my youth
  or my transgressions;
According to Your lovingkindness remember me,
For the sake of Your goodness, O Yahweh.
Good and upright is Yahweh;
Therefore He instructs sinners in the way.
May He lead the humble in justice,
And may He teach the humble His way.
All the paths of Yahweh are lovingkindness
  and truth
To those who guard His covenant
  and His testimonies.
For Your name's sake, O Yahweh,
Pardon my iniquity, for it is great.

Ps 139:23-24   Search me, O God, and know my heart;
Try me and know my anxious thoughts;
And see if there be any hurtful way in me,
And lead me in the everlasting way.

✍ **Pause to confess to God both your outward and inward transgressions**

As for me, I shall call upon God,
And Yahweh will save me.

Evening and morning and at noon,
    I will bring my complaint and moan,
And He will hear my voice.

1 Pet 1:3-5 Blessed be the God and Father of our Lord Jesus Christ, who according to His great mercy has caused me to be born again to a living hope through the resurrection of Jesus Christ from the dead, to obtain an inheritance incorruptible and undefiled and unfading, having been kept in heaven for me, one who is protected by the power of God through faith for a salvation ready to be revealed in the last time.

   📖 **Pause to affirm God's patience and His power**

DISCIPLES' Our Father who is in heaven,
PRAYER Hallowed be Your name.
Matt 6:9b-13 Your kingdom come. Your will be done,
    On earth as it is in heaven.
    Give us this day our daily bread.
    And forgive us our debts,
        as we also have forgiven our debtors.
    And do not lead us into temptation
        but deliver us from the evil one.
    For Yours is the kingdom and the power
        and the glory forever. Amen.

   📖 **Pause to meditate on the glorious power of the Father's kingdom**

PETITION
+Eph 4:29-32
May no unwholesome word proceed from my mouth, but only such a word as is good for building up what is needed, so that it will give grace to those who hear. And may I not grieve the Holy Spirit of God, by whom I was sealed for the day of redemption. May all bitterness and anger and wrath and shouting and slander be put away from me, along with all malice. Instead, may I be kind to others, tender-hearted, graciously forgiving others, just as God in Christ also has graciously forgiven me.

Ps 19:14
Let the words of my mouth
   and the meditation of my heart
Be acceptable in Your sight,
O Yahweh, my rock and my Redeemer.

  ౕ **Pause to ask God to guard your tongue**

INTERCESSION
+2 Chr 6:30-31
Listen from heaven Your dwelling place, and forgive, and give to each person according to all his ways, whose heart You know, for You alone know the hearts of the sons of men, that they may fear You, to walk in Your ways all the days they live upon the face of the land which You have given to our fathers.

  ౕ **Pause to intercede with God that reverent fear will characterize you and yours**

I will give thanks to You, O Lord,
    among the peoples;
I will sing praises to You among the nations.
For Your lovingkindness is great
    to the heavens
And Your truth to the skies.
Be exalted above the heavens, O God;
Let Your glory *be* above all the earth.

DAY 28

ADORATION

Ps 103:20-22

Bless Yahweh, you His angels,
Mighty in strength, who perform His word,
Obeying the voice of His word!
Bless Yahweh, all *you* His hosts,
You who serve Him, doing His will.
Bless Yahweh, all you works of His,
In all places of His rule;
Bless Yahweh, O my soul!

🔖 **Pause to adore your God and your Lamb**

THANKSGIVING

Ps 37:39-40

But the salvation of the righteous is from Yahweh;
He is their strength in time of distress.
Yahweh helps them and protects them;
He protects them from the wicked
    and saves them,
Because they take refuge in Him.

🔖 **Pause to give thanks to God for helping the weak,
including you**

CONFESSION

Ps 32:3-5

When I kept silent *about my sin*,
    my bones wasted away
Through my groaning all day long.
For day and night Your hand was heavy upon me;
My vitality was drained away
    as with the heat of summer.   Selah.

I acknowledged my sin to You,
And my iniquity I did not cover up;
I said, "I will confess my transgressions
　to Yahweh;"
And You forgave the iniquity of my sin.　Selah.

Ps 139:23-24 Search me, O God, and know my heart;
Try me and know my anxious thoughts;
And see if there be any hurtful way in me,
And lead me in the everlasting way.

↙ **Pause to confess to God your transgressions and relieve any guilt**

AFFIRMATION Though the fig tree should not blossom
Hab 3:17-19a And there be no produce on the vines,
Though the yield of the olive should fail
And the fields yield no food,
Though the flock should be cut off
　from the fold
And there be no cattle in the stalls,
Yet I will exult in Yahweh;
I will rejoice in the God of my salvation.
Yahweh, the Lord, is my strength,
And He has set my feet like hinds' *feet*
And makes me tread on my high places.

↙ **Pause to affirm that following God by faith is worth it**

Our Father who is in heaven,
Hallowed be Your name.
Your kingdom come. Your will be done,
On earth as it is in heaven.
Give us this day our daily bread.
And forgive us our debts,
    as we also have forgiven our debtors.
And do not lead us into temptation
    but deliver us from the evil one.
For Yours is the kingdom and the power
    and the glory forever. Amen.

🕊 **Pause to recognize that although God is in heaven**
He can still be addressed as your Father

PETITION
⁺Eph 1:17-19

I pray that the God of our Lord Jesus Christ,
the Father of glory, may give to me the Spirit of
wisdom and of revelation in the full knowledge
of Him, so that with the eyes of my heart
having been enlightened I will know what is
the hope of His calling, what are the riches
of the glory of His inheritance in the saints,
and what is the surpassing greatness of His
power toward me according to the working
of the might of His strength.

Ps 19:14

Let the words of my mouth
    and the meditation of my heart
Be acceptable in Your sight,
O Yahweh, my rock and my Redeemer.

> Pause to ask your God that spiritual wisdom be granted
> to your pastors and church leaders

INTERCESSION
+Matt 9:37b-38

The harvest is plentiful, but the workers are few. Therefore I pray earnestly to the Lord of the harvest to send out workers into His harvest.

John 4:35

Do you not say, "There are yet four months, and *then* comes the harvest"? Behold, I say to you, lift up your eyes and look on the fields, that they are white for harvest.

> Pause to intercede with God for the unsaved and
> missionaries who are reaching out to them

BENEDICTION
+Job 9:9-10

To the God who makes the Bear, Orion,
    and the Pleiades,
And the chambers of the south;
Who does great things, unsearchable,
And wondrous works, innumerable.

DAY 29

ADORATION *Amos 4:13*	For behold, He who forms mountains and creates the wind And declares to man what are His thoughts, He who makes dawn into gloom And treads on the high places of the earth, Yahweh God of hosts is His name.

🔖 **Pause to adore your God for His creative acts**

THANKSGIVING ⁺*Ps 107:8-9*	Let us give thanks to Yahweh for His lovingkindness, And for His wondrous deeds to the sons of men! For He has satisfied the thirsty soul, And the hungry soul He has filled with what is good.

🔖 **Pause to give thanks to God for His common grace on those who do not know Him**

CONFESSION ⁺*Ezra 9:6, 8*	O my God, I am ashamed and humiliated to lift up my face to You, my God, for my iniquities have multiplied above my head and my guilt has become great even to the heavens. But now for a brief moment grace has been shown from Yahweh our God, to enlighten my eyes and give me a little reviving in my slavery.

Ps 139:23-24	Search me, O God, and know my heart; Try me and know my anxious thoughts;

And see if there be any hurtful way in me,
And lead me in the everlasting way.

🕮 **Pause to confess to God your sins and rejoice in His mercy**

AFFIRMATION The words of Yahweh are pure words;
Ps 12:6-7 As silver tried in a furnace on the ground,
    refined seven times.
You, O Yahweh, will keep them;
You will guard him from this generation forever.

⁺*2 Tim 3:16-17* All Scripture is God-breathed and profitable for
teaching, for reproof, for correction, for training
in righteousness, so that I may be thoroughly
equipped for every good work.

🕮 **Pause to affirm the written and living Word of God**

DISCIPLES' Our Father who is in heaven,
PRAYER Hallowed be Your name.
Matt 6:9b-13 Your kingdom come. Your will be done,
On earth as it is in heaven.
Give us this day our daily bread.
And forgive us our debts,
    as we also have forgiven our debtors.
And do not lead us into temptation
    but deliver us from the evil one.
For Yours is the kingdom and the power
    and the glory forever. Amen.

✒ **Pause to recognize that your Father's "name" is more than a title but embodies all that He is**

PETITION I bow my knees before the Father, from whom
Eph 3:14-19 every family in heaven and on earth is named,
that He would give me, according to the riches
of His glory, to be strengthened with power
through His Spirit in the inner man, that Christ
may dwell in my heart through faith; and being
firmly rooted and grounded in love, I may be
able to comprehend with all the saints what is
the breadth and length and height and depth,
and to know the love of Christ which surpasses
knowledge, that I may be filled up to all the
fullness of God.

Ps 19:14 Let the words of my mouth
and the meditation of my heart
Be acceptable in Your sight,
O Yahweh, my rock and my Redeemer.

✒ **Pause to ask God for inner spiritual power and grace**

INTERCESSION May I not neglect to show hospitality to strangers,
Heb 13:2 for by this some have entertained angels without
knowing it.

Heb 13:3 I remember the prisoners, as though in prison
with them, and those who are mistreated.

🕊 **Pause to intercede with God for strangers in this country and in your life**

<table>
<tr><td>BENEDICTION</td><td>O Yahweh, Your name is everlasting,</td></tr>
<tr><td>*Ps 135:13, 21*</td><td>O Yahweh, Your remembrance is
    from generation to generation.
Blessed be Yahweh from Zion,
Who dwells in Jerusalem. Praise Yah!</td></tr>
</table>

2 Cor 13:14 The grace of the Lord Jesus Christ,
and the love of God, and the fellowship
of the Holy Spirit, be with you all.

DAY 30

ADORATION
Ps 63:1-3

O God, You are my God;
  I shall seek You earnestly;
My soul thirsts for You, my flesh yearns for You,
In a dry and weary land without water.
Thus I have beheld You in the sanctuary,
To see Your power and Your glory.
Because Your lovingkindness is better than life,
My lips will laud You.

Ps 3:8

Salvation belongs to Yahweh;
Your blessing *be* upon Your people!   Selah.

🖋 **Pause to adore your God for His saving grace**

THANKSGIVING
Ps 40:1-3

I hoped earnestly for Yahweh;
And He inclined to me and heard my cry for help.
He brought me up out of the pit of destruction,
    out of the miry clay,
And He set my feet upon a high rock,
He established my steps.
He put a new song in my mouth, a song
    of praise to our God;
Many will see and fear
And will trust in Yahweh.

🖋 **Pause to give thanks to God for rescuing you from
your foolishness**

The heart is more deceitful than all else
And is desperately sick;
Who can know it?
You, Yahweh, search the heart;
You test the inmost being,
Even to give to each man according to his ways,
According to the fruit of his deeds.

Ps 139:23-24 Search me, O God, and know my heart;
Try me and know my anxious thoughts;
And see if there be any hurtful way in me,
And lead me in the everlasting way.

⮎ **Pause to confess to God any sins of your heart**

AFFIRMATION
†2 Pet 1:19-21 I have as more sure the prophetic word, to which
I do well to pay attention as to a lamp shining
in a dark place, until the day dawns and the
morning star arises in my heart. I know this
first of all, that no prophecy of Scripture comes
by one's own interpretation. For no prophecy
was ever made by the will of man, but men
being moved by the Holy Spirit spoke from God.

Rom 15:4 For whatever was written in earlier times was
written for our instruction, so that through
the perseverance and the encouragement of
the Scriptures we might have hope.

⮎ **Pause to affirm the inspiration of God's Word**

Our Father who is in heaven,
Hallowed be Your name.
Your kingdom come. Your will be done,
On earth as it is in heaven.
Give us this day our daily bread.
And forgive us our debts,
    as we also have forgiven our debtors.
And do not lead us into temptation
    but deliver us from the evil one.
For Yours is the kingdom and the power
    and the glory forever. Amen.

🖎 **Pause to recognize how God's kingdom is both now and also yet to come**

In You, O Yahweh, I have taken refuge;
Let me never be ashamed;
In Your righteousness protect me.
Incline Your ear to me, deliver me quickly;
Be to me a rock of strength,
A fortress to save me.
For You are my high rock and my fortress;
For Your name's sake You will lead me and
    guide me.
You will bring me out of the net which
    they have secretly laid for me,
For You are my strength.
Into Your hand I commit my spirit;
You have ransomed me, O Yahweh, God of truth.

Col 3:23-24 Whatever I do, may I work heartily as for
the Lord rather than for men, knowing that
from the Lord I will receive the reward
of the inheritance. I serve the Lord Christ.

Ps 19:14 Let the words of my mouth
   and the meditation of my heart
Be acceptable in Your sight,
O Yahweh, my rock and my Redeemer.

⤺ **Pause to ask God that you will serve Him faithfully**

INTERCESSION O Yahweh, the God of Abraham, Isaac,
1 Chr 29:18 and Israel, our fathers, keep this forever
in the intentions of the heart of Your people,
and prepare their heart for You.

²2 Thess 3:1 Finally, I pray that the word of the Lord
will spread rapidly and be glorified.

⤺ **Pause to intercede with God for others, especially
the outreach of your local church**

BENEDICTION May Yahweh bless us, and keep us;
²Num 6:24-26 May Yahweh make His face shine on us,
And be gracious to us;
May Yahweh lift up His face on us,
And give us peace.

DAY 31

ADORATION

Ps 150
Praise Yah!
Praise God in His sanctuary;
Praise Him in His mighty expanse.
Praise Him for His mighty deeds;
Praise Him according to the abundance
of His greatness.
Praise Him with trumpet blast;
Praise Him with harp and lyre.
Praise Him with tambourine and dancing;
Praise Him with stringed instruments and pipe.
Praise Him with resounding cymbals;
Praise Him with clashing cymbals.
Let everything that has breath praise Yah.
Praise Yah!

꘎ **Pause to adore your God with every ounce of your being**

THANKSGIVING

Ps 89:1-2
I will sing of the lovingkindnesses
of Yahweh forever;
From generation to generation I will make known
Your faithfulness with my mouth.
For I have said, "Lovingkindness
will be built up forever;
In the heavens You will establish Your faithfulness."

⁺*1 Thess 5:18*
In everything I will give thanks, for this is God's
will for me in Christ Jesus.

✑ **Pause to give thanks to God for specific blessings**

CONFESSION
Ps 51:1-3

Be gracious to me, O God,
    according to Your lovingkindness;
According to the abundance of Your
    compassion blot out my transgressions.
Wash me thoroughly from my iniquity
And cleanse me from my sin.
For I know my transgressions,
And my sin is ever before me.

Ps 139:23-24

Search me, O God, and know my heart;
Try me and know my anxious thoughts;
And see if there be any hurtful way in me,
And lead me in the everlasting way.

✑ **Pause to confess to God any specific sins and shortcomings**

AFFIRMATION
1 Sam 2:9-10

He keeps the feet of His holy ones,
But the wicked ones are silenced in darkness,
For not by power shall a man prevail.
Those who contend with Yahweh
    will be dismayed;
Against them He will thunder in the heavens;
Yahweh will render justice to the ends
    of the earth,
And He will give strength to His king,
And He will exalt the horn of His anointed.

✑ **Pause to affirm God's justice in this unjust age**

Our Father who is in heaven,
Hallowed be Your name.
Your kingdom come. Your will be done,
On earth as it is in heaven.
Give us this day our daily bread.
And forgive us our debts,
    as we also have forgiven our debtors.
And do not lead us into temptation
    but deliver us from the evil one.
For Yours is the kingdom and the power
    and the glory forever. Amen.

✍ **Pause to delight in your Father's will in whatever way it is being shown to you**

Lord, I ask that I may be filled with the full knowledge of Your will in all spiritual wisdom and understanding, so that I may walk in a manner worthy of the Lord, to please You in all respects, bearing fruit in every good work and multiplying in the full knowledge of God. May I be strengthened with all power, according to Your glorious might, for the attaining of all steadfastness and patience; as I joyously give thanks to the Father, who has qualified me to share in the inheritance of the saints in light.

Ps 19:14 Let the words of my mouth
    and the meditation of my heart
Be acceptable in Your sight,
O Yahweh, my rock and my Redeemer.

🖋 **Pause to ask God to keep you humble, even if it hurts**

INTERCESSION
⁺*Eph 6:18-20* I am praying at all times with all prayer
and petition in the Spirit, and to this end,
being on the alert with all perseverance
and petition for all the saints, that words
may be given to them in the opening of
their mouths, to make known with boldness
the mystery of the gospel—for which I am
an ambassador—so that in proclaiming it
they may speak boldly, as they ought to speak.

🖋 **Pause to intercede with God for missionaries and ministers**

BENEDICTION
Ps 72:18-19 Blessed be Yahweh God, the God of Israel,
Who alone works wondrous deeds.
And blessed be His glorious name forever;
And may the whole earth be filled
    with His glory.
Amen, and Amen.

Is 12:1-5 I will give thanks to You, O Yahweh;
For although You were angry with me,
Your anger is turned away,
And You comfort me. Behold, God is my salvation,
I will trust and not dread;
For Yah—Yahweh Himself—is my strength and song,
And He has become my salvation.
Therefore I will joyously draw water
From the springs of salvation.
And in that day I will say,
"Give thanks to Yahweh, call on His name.
Make known His deeds among the peoples;
Make them remember that His name is exalted."
Praise Yahweh in song,
for He has done majestic things;
Let this be known throughout the earth.

Eph 2:8-9 For by grace I have been saved through faith,
and this is not of myself, it is the gift of God; not
of works, so that no one may boast. For I am His
workmanship, created in Christ Jesus for good works,
which God prepared beforehand so that
I would walk in them.

2 Thess 3:5 May the Lord direct my heart into the love of
God and into the steadfastness of Christ.

PRAYING
SCRIPTURE

———

FOR A WEEK

ADORATION

Ps 96:1-6

Sing to Yahweh a new song;
Sing to Yahweh, all the earth.
Sing to Yahweh, bless His name;
Proclaim good news of His salvation
    from day to day.
Recount His glory among the nations,
His wondrous deeds among all the peoples.
For great is Yahweh and greatly to be praised;
He is more fearsome than all gods.
For all the gods of the peoples are idols,
But Yahweh made the heavens.
Splendor and majesty are before Him,
Strength and beauty are in His sanctuary.

Rev 15:3-4

And they sang the song of Moses, the slave
of God, and the song of the Lamb, saying,
    "GREAT AND MARVELOUS ARE YOUR WORKS,
    O LORD GOD, THE ALMIGHTY;
    RIGHTEOUS AND TRUE ARE YOUR WAYS,
    KING OF THE NATIONS!
    WHO WILL NOT FEAR, O LORD,
        AND GLORIFY YOUR NAME?
    For You alone are holy;
    For ALL THE NATIONS WILL COME
        AND WORSHIP BEFORE YOU,
    FOR YOUR RIGHTEOUS ACTS
        HAVE BEEN REVEALED."

THANKSGIVING   I will rejoice greatly in Yahweh;
Is 61:10-11   My soul will rejoice in my God,
For He has clothed me with garments of salvation,
He has wrapped me with a robe of righteousness,
As a bridegroom decks himself with a headdress,
And as a bride adorns herself with her jewels.
For as the earth brings forth its branches,
And as a garden causes the things sown in it
   to branch out,
So Lord Yahweh will cause righteousness and praise
To branch out before all the nations.

Ps 62:1-2   Surely my soul *waits* in silence for God;
From Him is my salvation.
Surely He is my rock and my salvation,
My stronghold; I shall not be greatly shaken.

Pause to give thanks to God for specific tokens of His kindness

CONFESSION   Be gracious to me, O God,
Ps 51:1-10,   according to Your lovingkindness;
12-13   According to the abundance of Your compassion
      blot out my transgressions.
Wash me thoroughly from my iniquity
And cleanse me from my sin.
For I know my transgressions,
And my sin is ever before me.
Against You, You only, I have sinned

And done what is evil in Your sight,
So that You are justified when You speak
And pure when You judge.
Behold, I was brought forth in iniquity,
And in sin my mother conceived me.
Behold, You delight in truth
   in the innermost being,
And in the hidden part You will make me
   know wisdom.
Purify me with hyssop, and I shall be clean;
Wash me, and I shall be whiter than snow.
Make me to hear joy and gladness,
Let the bones which You have crushed rejoice.
Hide Your face from my sins
And blot out all my iniquities.
Create in me a clean heart, O God,
And renew a steadfast spirit within me.
Restore to me the joy of Your salvation
And sustain me with a willing spirit.
Then I will teach transgressors Your ways,
And sinners will be converted to You.

Ps 139:23-24 Search me, O God, and know my heart;
Try me and know my anxious thoughts;
And see if there be any hurtful way in me,
And lead me in the everlasting way.

  🕮 **Pause to confess to God sins that are hidden from others**

I will not store up for myself treasures on earth, where moth and rust destroy, and where thieves break in and steal. But I will store up treasures in heaven, where neither moth nor rust destroys, and where thieves do not break in or steal; for I know that where my treasure is, there my heart will be also.

2 Cor 5:9-10 Therefore we also have as our ambition, whether at home or absent, to be pleasing to Him. For we must all appear before the judgment seat of Christ, so that each one may be recompensed for his deeds in the body, according to what he has done, whether good or bad.

🔖 **Pause to affirm God's provisions for all your needs**

DISCIPLES'
PRAYER
Matt 6:9b-13   Our Father who is in heaven,
Hallowed be Your name.
Your kingdom come. Your will be done,
On earth as it is in heaven.
Give us this day our daily bread.
And forgive us our debts,
    as we also have forgiven our debtors.
And do not lead us into temptation
    but deliver us from the evil one.
For Yours is the kingdom and the power
    and the glory forever. Amen.

🔖 **Pause to reflect on how your Father's will in heaven can be realized on earth**

Is 58:6-9a

Is this not the fast which You choose,
To loosen the bonds of wickedness,
To release the bands of the yoke,
And to let the oppressed go free
And break every yoke?
Is it not to divide our bread with the hungry
And bring the afflicted homeless into the house;
When we see the naked, we cover him;
And not to hide ourselves from our own flesh?
Then our light will break out like the dawn,
And our recovery will speedily spring forth;
And our righteousness will go before us;
The glory of Yahweh will be our rear guard.
Then we will call, and Yahweh will answer;
We will cry, and He will say, "Here I am."

Phil 2:3-4

May I do nothing from selfish ambition or
vain glory, but with humility of mind regard
one another as more important than myself,
not *merely* looking out for my own personal
interests, but also for the interests of others.

Ps 19:14

Let the words of my mouth
    and the meditation of my heart
Be acceptable in Your sight,
O Yahweh, my rock and my Redeemer.

> Pause to intercede with God about looking out for others over yourself

INTERCESSION
+Col 4:2-6

May I devote myself to prayer, being watchful
in it with thanksgiving; praying at the same time
as well that God will open up to me a door
for the word, so that I may speak the mystery
of Christ, for which I have also been bound,
that I may make it manifest in the way I ought
to speak. May I walk in wisdom toward outsiders,
redeeming the time. Let my words always be
with grace, seasoned with salt, so that I will
know how I should answer each person.

+Eph 6:19-20

May words be given to me in the opening
of my mouth, to make known with boldness
the mystery of the gospel—for which I am an
ambassador—so that in *proclaiming* it I may
speak boldly, as I ought to speak.

✎ **Pause to intercede with God about non-believers**

BENEDICTION
Ps 72:17-19

May his name endure forever;
May his name increase as long as the sun *shines*;
Let *all nations* be blessed in him;
Let all nations call him blessed.
Blessed be Yahweh God, the God of Israel,
Who alone works wondrous deeds.
And blessed be His glorious name forever;
And may the whole earth be filled with His glory.
Amen, and Amen.

ADORATION

Ps 150

Praise Yah!
Praise God in His sanctuary;
Praise Him in His mighty expanse.
Praise Him for His mighty deeds;
Praise Him according to the abundance
    of His greatness.
Praise Him with trumpet blast;
Praise Him with harp and lyre.
Praise Him with tambourine and dancing;
Praise Him with stringed instruments and pipe.
Praise Him with resounding cymbals;
Praise Him with clashing cymbals.
Let everything that has breath praise Yah.
Praise Yah!

Pause to behold your God

THANKSGIVING

2 Sam 22:2b-4

Yahweh is my rock and my fortress
    and my deliverer;
My God, my rock, in whom I take refuge,
My shield and the horn of my salvation,
    my stronghold and my refuge;
My savior, You save me from violence.
I call upon Yahweh, who is worthy
    to be praised,
And I am saved from my enemies.

Ps 4:7-8   You have put gladness in my heart,
            More than when their grain and new wine abound.
            In peace I will both lie down and sleep,
            For You alone, O Yahweh, make me to abide
                in safety.

🖋   **Pause to give thanks to God for specific blessings**

CONFESSION   Remember, O Yahweh, Your compassion
Ps 25:6-11   and Your lovingkindnesses,
              For they have been from of old.
              Do not remember the sins of my youth
                  or my transgressions;
              According to Your lovingkindness remember me,
              For the sake of Your goodness, O Yahweh.
              Good and upright is Yahweh;
              Therefore He instructs sinners in the way.
              May He lead the humble in justice,
              And may He teach the humble His way.
              All the paths of Yahweh are lovingkindness
                  and truth
              To those who guard His covenant and His
                  testimonies.
              For Your name's sake, O Yahweh,
              Pardon my iniquity, for it is great.

Ps 139:23-24   Search me, O God, and know my heart;
               Try me and know my anxious thoughts;
               And see if there be any hurtful way in me,
               And lead me in the everlasting way.

✎ **Pause to confess to God specific sins that come to mind**

AFFIRMATION
⁺2 Tim 3:16-17
All Scripture is God-breathed and profitable for teaching, for reproof, for correction, for training in righteousness, so that I may be thoroughly equipped for every good work.

⁺1 Pet 1:3-5
Blessed be the God and Father of our Lord Jesus Christ, who according to His great mercy has caused me to be born again to a living hope through the resurrection of Jesus Christ from the dead, to *obtain* an inheritance incorruptible and undefiled and unfading, having been kept in heaven for me, one who is protected by the power of God through faith for a salvation ready to be revealed in the last time.

✎ **Pause to affirm God's Word and His salvation**

DISCIPLES'
PRAYER
Matt 6:9b-13
Our Father who is in heaven,
Hallowed be Your name.
Your kingdom come. Your will be done,
On earth as it is in heaven.
Give us this day our daily bread.
And forgive us our debts,
    as we also have forgiven our debtors.
And do not lead us into temptation
    but deliver us from the evil one.
For Yours is the kingdom and the power
    and the glory forever. Amen.

> 🍃 **Pause to be grateful for Israel's daily manna and your daily food**

PETITION
⁺Eph 4:29-32

May no unwholesome word proceed from my mouth, but only such *a word* as is good for building up what is needed, so that it will give grace to those who hear. And may I not grieve the Holy Spirit of God, by whom I was sealed for the day of redemption. May all bitterness and anger and wrath and shouting and slander be put away from me, along with all malice. Instead, may I be kind to others, tender-hearted, graciously forgiving others, just as God in Christ also has graciously forgiven me.

⁺2 Thess 3:5

May the Lord direct my heart into the love of God and into the steadfastness of Christ.

Ps 19:14

Let the words of my mouth
 and the meditation of my heart
Be acceptable in Your sight,
O Yahweh, my rock and my Redeemer.

> 🍃 **Pause to ask God about your personal needs, both physical and spiritual**

INTERCESSION
⁺1 Tim 2:1-4

First of all, then, I offer petitions *and* prayers, requests *and* thanksgivings, for all men, for kings and all who are in authority, so that I may lead a tranquil and quiet life in all godliness and dignity.

This is good and acceptable in the sight of God our Savior, who desires all men to be saved and to come to the full knowledge of the truth.

Matt 9:37b-38 The harvest is plentiful, but the workers are few. Therefore I pray earnestly to the Lord of the harvest to send out workers into His harvest.

🖐 **Pause to intercede with God for those in authority in local and national governments**

BENEDICTION Yahweh bless us, and keep us;
Num 6:24-26 Yahweh make His face shine on us,
And be gracious to us;
Yahweh lift up His face on us,
And give us peace.

ADORATION

Ps 63:1-5

O God, You are my God;
I shall seek You earnestly;
My soul thirsts for You, my flesh yearns for You,
In a dry and weary land without water.
Thus I have beheld You in the sanctuary,
To see Your power and Your glory.
Because Your lovingkindness is better than life,
My lips will laud You.
Thus I will bless You as long as I live;
I will lift up my hands in Your name.
My soul is satisfied as with fatness and richness,
And my mouth offers praises with lips of
joyful songs.

✍ **Pause to adore your God**

THANKSGIVING

Ps 89:1-2

I will sing of the lovingkindnesses
of Yahweh forever;
From generation to generation I will make
known Your faithfulness with my mouth.
For I have said, "Lovingkindness
will be built up forever;
In the heavens You will establish
Your faithfulness."

⁺Ps 107:8-9

Let us give thanks to Yahweh for His lovingkindness,
And for His wondrous deeds to the sons of men!

For He has satisfied the thirsty soul,
And the hungry soul He has filled
    with what is good.

    ⌇ **Pause to give thanks to God for specific blessings**

CONFESSION To You, O Lord, belongs righteousness, but to
⁺Dan 9:7, 17 me open shame, as it is this day—because of my
unfaithful deeds which I have committed against
You. So now, my God, listen to the prayer of Your
slave and to my supplications, and for Your
sake, O Lord, let Your face shine on me again.

⁺Jon 4:2b I know that You are a gracious and compassionate
God, slow to anger and abundant in lovingkindness, and one who relents concerning evil.

1 John 1:8-9 If we say that we have no sin, we deceive
ourselves and the truth is not in us. If we
confess our sins, He is faithful and righteous
to forgive us our sins and to cleanse us
from all unrighteousness.

Ps 139:23-24 Search me, O God, and know my heart;
Try me and know my anxious thoughts;
And see if there be any hurtful way in me,
And lead me in the everlasting way.

    ⌇ **Pause to confess to God any specific sins that are coming to mind**

AFFIRMATION
Ps 1:1a, 2-3

How blessed is the one
Whose delight is in the law of Yahweh,
And in His law he meditates day and night.
And he will be like a tree *firmly* planted
    by streams of water,
Which yields its fruit in its season
And its leaf does not wither;
And in whatever he does, he prospers.

Ps 119:97

Oh how I love Your law!
It is my meditation all the day.

⁺*2 Pet 1:19-21*

I have as more sure the prophetic word, to which
I do well to pay attention as to a lamp shining in a
dark place, until the day dawns and the morning
star arises in my heart. I know this first of all, that
no prophecy of Scripture comes by one's own
interpretation. For no prophecy was ever made by
the will of man, but men being moved by the Holy
Spirit spoke from God.

   ↅ **Pause to affirm God's truth in His inspired Word**

DISCIPLES'
PRAYER
Matt 6:9b-13

Our Father who is in heaven,
Hallowed be Your name.
Your kingdom come. Your will be done,
On earth as it is in heaven.
Give us this day our daily bread.
And forgive us our debts,
    as we also have forgiven our debtors.

And do not lead us into temptation
　　but deliver us from the evil one.
For Yours is the kingdom and the power
　　and the glory forever. Amen.

↫ **Pause to decide how you can show to others the Father's mercy shown to you**

PETITION
Ps 27:7-8

Hear, O Yahweh, when I call with my voice,
And be gracious to me and answer me.
On Your *behalf* my heart says, "Seek My face,"
"Your face, O Yahweh, I shall seek."

⁺*1 Pet 3:8-9*

May I and my fellow believers be like-minded,
sympathetic, brotherly, tender-hearted, and
humble in spirit; not returning evil for evil
or reviling for reviling, but giving a blessing
instead, for we were called for the very purpose
that we might inherit a blessing.

Ps 19:14

Let the words of my mouth
　　and the meditation of my heart
Be acceptable in Your sight,
O Yahweh, my rock and my Redeemer.

↫ **Pause to ask God about your personal needs, especially greater compassion and care for others**

INTERCESSION
⁺*Col 4:2-4*

I devote myself to prayer, being watchful in it
with thanksgiving; praying at the same time

that God will open up to me a door for the word, so that I may speak the mystery of Christ, for which I may also be bound, that I may make it manifest in the way I ought to speak.

Eph 6:18-19 I pray at all times with all prayer and petition in the Spirit, and to this end, being on the alert with all perseverance and petition for all the saints, that words may be given to me in the opening of my mouth, to make known with boldness the mystery of the gospel.

> ↳ **Pause to intercede with God for others to be bold in their witness**

BENEDICTION
1 Kin 8:56-60 Blessed be Yahweh, who has given rest to His people, according to all that He promised; not one promise has failed of all His good promises, which He promised by the hand of Moses His servant. May Yahweh our God be with us, as He was with our fathers; may He not forsake us or abandon us, that He may incline our hearts to Himself, to walk in all His ways and to keep His commandments and His statutes and His judgments, which He commanded our fathers. And may these words of mine, with which I have made supplication before Yahweh, be near to Yahweh our God day and night, that He may do justice for His slave and justice for His people, as each day requires, so that all the peoples of the earth may know that Yahweh is God; there is no one else.

❧WEDNESDAY❧

ADORATION

Ps 139:1-6
O Yahweh, You have searched me and known *me*.
You know when I sit down and when I rise up;
You understand my thought from afar.
You scrutinize my path and my lying down,
And are intimately acquainted with all my ways.
Even before there is a word on my tongue,
Behold, O Yahweh, You know it all.
You have enclosed me behind and before,
And You have put Your hand upon me.
Such knowledge is too wonderful for me;
It is *too* high, I cannot attain to it.

🍃 **Pause to adore your God**

THANKSGIVING

Ps 40:1-3
I hoped earnestly for Yahweh;
And He inclined to me and heard my cry for help.
He brought me up out of the pit of destruction,
    out of the miry clay,
And He set my feet upon a high rock,
    He established my steps.
He put a new song in my mouth,
    a song of praise to our God;
Many will see and fear
And will trust in Yahweh.

Ps 34:6-7 This poor man called out, and Yahweh heard him
And saved him out of all his troubles.
The angel of Yahweh encamps
    around those who fear Him,
And rescues them.

ᴊ **Pause to give thanks to God for specific blessings**

CONFESSION How blessed is he whose transgression is forgiven,
Ps 32:1-5 Whose sin is covered!
How blessed is the man whose iniquity Yahweh
    will not take into account,
And in whose spirit there is no deceit!
When I kept silent *about my sin*,
    my bones wasted away
Through my groaning all day long.
For day and night Your hand was heavy upon me;
My vitality was drained away
    as with the heat of summer.   Selah.
I acknowledged my sin to You,
And my iniquity I did not cover up;
I said, "I will confess my transgressions to Yahweh;"
And You forgave the iniquity of my sin.   Selah.

Ps 139:23-24 Search me, O God, and know my heart;
Try me and know my anxious thoughts;
And see if there be any hurtful way in me,
And lead me in the everlasting way.

🕮 Pause to confess to God any transgressions of which you are aware

AFFIRMATION

Hab 2:4

Behold, as for the proud one,
His soul is not right within him;
But the righteous will live by his faith.

Hab 3:17-19a

Though the fig tree should not blossom
And there be no produce on the vines,
Though the yield of the olive should fail
And the fields yield no food,
Though the flock should be cut off from the fold
And there be no cattle in the stalls,
Yet I will exult in Yahweh;
I will rejoice in the God of my salvation.
Yahweh, the Lord, is my strength,
And He has set my feet like hinds' *feet*
And makes me tread on my high places.

🕮 Pause to affirm God's truth

DISCIPLES'
PRAYER

Matt 6:9b-13

Our Father who is in heaven,
Hallowed be Your name.
Your kingdom come. Your will be done,
On earth as it is in heaven.
Give us this day our daily bread.
And forgive us our debts,
    as we also have forgiven our debtors.
And do not lead us into temptation

but deliver us from the evil one.
For Yours is the kingdom and the power
    and the glory forever. Amen.

🖋 **Pause to pray for your spiritual armor so you can resist the devil's schemes**

PETITION

Ps 16:1-6

Keep me, O God, for I take refuge in You.
O my soul, you have said to Yahweh,
    "You are my Lord;
I have no good without You."
As for the saints who are in the earth,
They are the majestic ones in whom is all
    my delight.
The pains of those who have bartered
    for another *god* will be multiplied;
I shall not pour out their drink offerings of blood,
Nor will I take their names upon my lips.
Yahweh is the portion of my inheritance and my cup;
You support my lot.
The lines have fallen to me in pleasant places;
Indeed, my inheritance is beautiful to me.

Ps 19:14

Let the words of my mouth
    and the meditation of my heart
Be acceptable in Your sight,
O Yahweh, my rock and my Redeemer.

🖋 **Pause to ask God about your personal needs, especially your ministry in church**

Salvation belongs to Yahweh;
Ps 3:8 Your blessing *be* upon Your people!   Selah.

⁺Heb 13:16 May I not neglect doing good and sharing,
for with such sacrifices God is pleased.

⁺1 Thess Now may our God and Father Himself and
3:11-12 Jesus our Lord direct our way, and may the
Lord cause us to increase and abound in love
for one another, and for all people, just as
we also *do* for others.

🕮 **Pause to intercede for unity and peace in your local
church and wisdom for the leaders**

BENEDICTION Now the God of peace, who brought up from
⁺Heb 13:20-21 the dead the great Shepherd of the sheep
through the blood of the eternal covenant,
our Lord Jesus, equip us in every good thing
to do His will, by doing in us what is pleasing
in His sight, through Jesus Christ, to whom *be*
the glory forever and ever. Amen.

⁺2 Cor 13:14 The grace of the Lord Jesus Christ, and the love
of God, and the fellowship of the Holy Spirit,
be with us all.

⇥ THURSDAY ⇤

ADORATION

Ps 139:7-12
Where can I go from Your Spirit?
Or where can I flee from Your presence?
If I ascend to heaven, You are there;
If I make my bed in Sheol, behold, You are there.
If I lift up the wings of the dawn,
If I dwell in the remotest part of the sea,
Even there Your hand will lead me,
And Your right hand will lay hold of me.
If I say, "Surely the darkness will bruise me,
And the light around me will be night,"
Even the darkness is not too dark for You,
And the night is as bright as the day.
Darkness and light are alike *to You.*

🖌 **Pause to behold your God**

THANKSGIVING

Ps 139:13-18
For You formed my inward parts;
You wove me in my mother's womb.
I will give thanks to You, for I am fearfully
   and wonderfully made;
Wonderful are Your works,
And my soul knows it very well.
My frame was not hidden from You,
When I was made in secret,
And intricately woven in the depths of the earth;
Your eyes have seen my unshaped substance;

And in Your book all of them were written
The days that were formed *for me*,
When as yet there was not one of them.
How precious are Your thoughts to me, O God!
How vast is the sum of them!
If I should count them,
    they would outnumber the sand.
When I awake, I am still with You.

1 Cor 15:57-58   But thanks be to God, who gives us the victory
through our Lord Jesus Christ! Therefore,
my beloved brothers, be steadfast, immovable,
always abounding in the work of the Lord,
knowing that your labor is not *in* vain
in the Lord.

    ꒊ **Pause to give thanks to God for some specific blessings**

CONFESSION   Create in me a clean heart, O God,
Ps 51:10-15   And renew a steadfast spirit within me.
Do not cast me away from Your presence
And do not take Your Holy Spirit from me.
Restore to me the joy of Your salvation
And sustain me with a willing spirit.
Then I will teach transgressors Your ways,
And sinners will be converted to You.
Deliver me from bloodguiltiness, O God,
    the God of my salvation;

Then my tongue will joyfully sing
    of Your righteousness.
O Lord, open my lips,
That my mouth may declare Your praise.

Ps 139:23-24   Search me, O God, and know my heart;
Try me and know my anxious thoughts;
And see if there be any hurtful way in me,
And lead me in the everlasting way.

↳ **Pause to confess to God any sins that are becoming evident in your life**

AFFIRMATION The God who made the world and all things in it,
Acts 17:24-28a since He is Lord of heaven and earth, does not dwell in temples made with hands; nor is He served by human hands, as though He needed anything, since He Himself gives to all *people* life and breath and all things; and He made from one *man* every nation of mankind to inhabit all the face of the earth, having determined *their* appointed times and the boundaries of their habitation, that they would seek God, if perhaps they might grope for Him and find Him, though He is not far from each one of us; for in Him we live and move and exist.

John 4:24   God is spirit, and those who worship Him must worship in spirit and truth.

↳ **Pause to affirm God's truth**

Our Father who is in heaven,
Hallowed be Your name.
Matt 6:9b-13 Your kingdom come. Your will be done,
On earth as it is in heaven.
Give us this day our daily bread.
And forgive us our debts,
    as we also have forgiven our debtors.
And do not lead us into temptation
    but deliver us from the evil one.
For Yours is the kingdom and the power
    and the glory forever. Amen.

⮌ **Pause to meditate on the glorious power of the Father's kingdom**

PETITION Keep my soul and deliver me;
Ps 25:20-21 Do not let me be ashamed,
    for I take refuge in You.
Let integrity and uprightness guard me,
For I hope in You.

Ps 31:1-5 In You, O Yahweh, I have taken refuge;
Let me never be ashamed;
In Your righteousness protect me.
Incline Your ear to me, deliver me quickly;
Be to me a rock of strength,
A fortress to save me.
For You are my high rock and my fortress;

For Your name's sake You will lead me
    and guide me.
You will bring me out of the net
    which they have secretly laid for me,
For You are my strength.
Into Your hand I commit my spirit;
You have ransomed me, O Yahweh, God of truth.

Ps 19:14 Let the words of my mouth
    and the meditation of my heart
Be acceptable in Your sight,
O Yahweh, my rock and my Redeemer.

🖋 **Pause to ask God about your personal needs**

INTERCESSION I am Yahweh, I have called You in righteousness;
Is 42:6-7 I will also take hold of You by the hand
    and guard You,
And I will give You as a covenant to the people,
As a light to the nations,
To open blind eyes,
To bring out prisoners from the dungeon
And those who inhabit darkness from the prison.

Heb 13:2-3a May I not neglect to show hospitality to strangers,
for by this some have entertained angels without
knowing it. I remember the prisoners, as though
in prison with them, *and* those who are mistreated.

〜 **Pause to intercede with God for service personnel and prisoners and their chaplains**

BENEDICTION
Ps 72:18-19

Blessed be Yahweh God, the God of Israel,
Who alone works wondrous deeds.
And blessed be His glorious name forever;
And may the whole earth be filled
    with His glory.
Amen, and Amen.

FRIDAY

ADORATION

Ps 42:1-5
As the deer pants for the water brooks,
So my soul pants for You, O God.
My soul thirsts for God, for the living God;
When shall I come and appear before God?
My tears have been my food day and night,
While *they* say to me all day long,
"Where is your God?"
These things I remember and I pour out my soul
within me.
For I used to go along with the throng *and* lead
them in procession to the house of God,
With the sound of a shout of joy and thanksgiving,
a multitude keeping festival.
Why are you in despair, O my soul?
And *why* are you disturbed within me?
Wait for God, for I shall still praise Him,
For the salvation of His presence.

Pause to adore your God

THANKSGIVING

Ps 103:1-5
Bless Yahweh, O my soul,
And all that is within me, *bless* His holy name.
Bless Yahweh, O my soul,
And forget none of His benefits;
Who pardons all your iniquities,
Who heals all your diseases;
Who redeems your life from the pit,

Who crowns you with lovingkindness
   and compassion;
Who satisfies your years with good things,
So that your youth is renewed like the eagle.

†1 Thess 5:18 In everything I will give thanks, for this is God's
will for me in Christ Jesus.

🕊 **Pause to give thanks to God for specific blessings**

CONFESSION When I kept silent *about my sin,*
Ps 32:3-5   my bones wasted away
Through my groaning all day long.
For day and night Your hand was heavy upon me;
My vitality was drained away
   as with the heat of summer.   Selah.
I acknowledged my sin to You,
And my iniquity I did not cover up;
I said, "I will confess my transgressions
   to Yahweh;"
And You forgave the iniquity of my sin.   Selah.

Ps 139:23-24 Search me, O God, and know my heart;
Try me and know my anxious thoughts;
And see if there be any hurtful way in me,
And lead me in the everlasting way.

🕊 **Pause to confess to God any specific sins that are causing
you to stumble**

As for God, His way is blameless;
The word of Yahweh is tried;
He is a shield to all who take refuge in Him.
For who is God, but Yahweh?
And who is a rock, except our God,
The God who girds me with strength
And makes my way blameless?

Is 57:15   For thus says the One high and lifted up
Who dwells forever, whose name is Holy,
"I dwell *on* a high and holy place,
And *also* with the crushed and lowly of spirit
In order to revive the spirit of the lowly
And to revive the heart of the crushed."

✍ **Pause to thank Him that in Jesus He is both high and holy and meek and lowly**

DISCIPLES'
PRAYER
Matt 6:9b-13

Our Father who is in heaven,
Hallowed be Your name.
Your kingdom come. Your will be done,
On earth as it is in heaven.
Give us this day our daily bread.
And forgive us our debts,
     as we also have forgiven our debtors.
And do not lead us into temptation
     but deliver us from the evil one.
For Yours is the kingdom and the power
     and the glory forever. Amen.

🍃 **Pause to recognize that although God is in heaven He can still be addressed as your Father**

PETITION

Ps 143:7-9

Answer me quickly, O Yahweh,
my spirit wastes away;
Do not hide Your face from me,
Or I will become like those who go down
to the pit.
Cause me to hear Your lovingkindness
in the morning;
For I trust in You;
Cause me to know the way in which
I should walk;
For to You I lift up my soul.
Deliver me from my enemies, O Yahweh,
I have concealed *myself* in You.

⁺*Col 3:23-24*

Whatever I do, may I work heartily, as for
the Lord rather than for men, knowing that
from the Lord I will receive the reward
of the inheritance. I serve the Lord Christ.

⁺*Phil 2:3-4*

May I do nothing from selfish ambition or
vain glory, but with humility of mind regard
others as more important than myself, not
merely looking out for my own personal
interests, but also for the interests of others.

Ps 19:14 Let the words of my mouth
and the meditation of my heart
Be acceptable in Your sight,
O Yahweh, my rock and my Redeemer.

🖉 **Pause to ask God about your personal needs**

INTERCESSION Salvation belongs to Yahweh;
Ps 3:8 Your blessing *be* upon Your people!   Selah.

⁺1 Tim 2:1-4 First of all, then, I offer petitions *and* prayers,
requests *and* thanksgivings, for all men, for kings
and all who are in authority, so that I may lead a
tranquil and quiet life in all godliness and dignity.
This is good and acceptable in the sight of God
our Savior, who desires all men to be saved and to
come to the full knowledge of the truth.

⁺Heb 13:16 May I not neglect doing good and sharing,
for with such sacrifices God is pleased.

🖉 **Pause to intercede with God for others, especially pastors
and Christian workers**

BENEDICTION Now to Him who is able to keep us from stumbling,
⁺Jude 24-25 and to make us stand in the presence of His glory
blameless with great joy, to the only God our Savior,
through Jesus Christ our Lord, *be* glory, majesty,
might, and authority, before all time and now and
forever. Amen.

ADORATION
Ps 63:4b-8

I will lift up my hands in Your name.
My soul is satisfied as with fatness and richness,
And my mouth offers praises with lips
    of joyful songs.
When I remember You on my bed,
I meditate on You in the night watches,
For You have been my help,
And in the shadow of Your wings I sing for joy.
My soul clings to You;
Your right hand upholds me.

✍ **Pause to behold your God**

THANKSGIVING
Ps 100

Make a loud shout to Yahweh, all the earth.
Serve Yahweh with gladness;
Come before Him with joyful songs.
Know that Yahweh, He is God;
It is He who has made us, and not we ourselves;
We are His people and the sheep of His pasture.
Enter His gates with thanksgiving
And His courts with praise.
Give thanks to Him, bless His name.
For Yahweh is good;
His lovingkindness endures forever
And His faithfulness, generation
    unto generation.

✍ **Pause to give thanks to God for specific blessings**

CONFESSION

Ps 25:6-11

Remember, O Yahweh, Your compassion
   and Your lovingkindnesses,
For they have been from of old.
Do not remember the sins of my youth
   or my transgressions;
According to Your lovingkindness remember me,
For the sake of Your goodness, O Yahweh.
Good and upright is Yahweh;
Therefore He instructs sinners in the way.
May He lead the humble in justice,
And may He teach the humble His way.
All the paths of Yahweh are lovingkindness
   and truth
To those who guard His covenant
   and His testimonies.
For Your name's sake, O Yahweh,
Pardon my iniquity, for it is great.

Ps 139:23-24

Search me, O God, and know my heart;
Try me and know my anxious thoughts;
And see if there be any hurtful way in me,
And lead me in the everlasting way.

✍ **Pause to confess to God any "favorite" sins that you know are slowing down your race**

Yahweh is my God, Yahweh is one! I will love
Yahweh my God with all my heart and with
all my soul and with all my might.

Ps 55:16-17 As for me, I shall call upon God,
And Yahweh will save me.
Evening and morning and at noon,
  I will bring my complaint and moan,
And He will hear my voice.

Ps 18:6 In my distress I called upon Yahweh,
And cried to my God for help;
He heard my voice out of His temple,
And my cry for help before Him came
  into His ears.

✍ **Pause to affirm these truths about God and that He
hears us**

DISCIPLES'
PRAYER
Matt 6:9b-13 Our Father who is in heaven,
Hallowed be Your name.
Your kingdom come. Your will be done,
On earth as it is in heaven.
Give us this day our daily bread.
And forgive us our debts,
  as we also have forgiven our debtors.
And do not lead us into temptation
  but deliver us from the evil one.
For Yours is the kingdom and the power
  and the glory forever. Amen.

᪐ **Pause to recognize that your Father's "name" is more than a title but embodies all that He is**

PETITION
Ps 86:11-12

Teach me Your way, O Yahweh;
I will walk in Your truth;
Unite my heart to fear Your name.
I will give thanks to You, O Lord my God,
    with all my heart,
And will glorify Your name forever.

⁺Heb 4:14-16

Therefore, since I have a great high priest who
has passed through the heavens, Jesus the Son of
God, I take hold of my confession. For I do not
have a high priest who cannot sympathize with
my weaknesses, but One who has been tempted
in all things like *I am, yet* without sin. Therefore I
draw near with confidence to the throne of grace,
so that I may receive mercy and find grace to help
in my time of need.

Ps 19:14

Let the words of my mouth
    and the meditation of my heart
Be acceptable in Your sight,
O Yahweh, my rock and my Redeemer.

᪐ **Pause to ask God about your personal needs**

INTERCESSION
⁺Matt 9:37b-
38

The harvest is plentiful, but the workers are few.
Therefore I pray earnestly to the Lord of the harvest
to send out workers into His harvest.

1 Pet 3:8-9 May I and my fellow believers be like-minded, sympathetic, brotherly, tender-hearted, and humble in spirit; not returning evil for evil or reviling for reviling, but giving a blessing instead, for we were called for the very purpose that we might inherit a blessing.

1 Thess 3:11-12 Now may our God and Father Himself and Jesus our Lord direct our way, and may the Lord cause us to increase and abound in love for one another, and for all people, just as we also *do* for others.

⤺ **Pause to intercede for others facing difficulties in their marriage and with their children**

BENEDICTION
Num 6:24-26 May Yahweh bless us, and keep us;
May Yahweh make His face shine on us,
And be gracious to us;
May Yahweh lift up His face on us,
And give us peace.

⁺Eph 2:8-9 For by grace I have been saved through faith,
and this is not of myself, *it is* the gift of God;
not of works, so that no one may boast.
For I am His workmanship, created in Christ Jesus
for good works, which God prepared beforehand
so that I would walk in them.

⁺2 Thess 3:5 May the Lord direct my heart into the love of God
and into the steadfastness of Christ.

APPENDIX
ONE

PRAYERS FROM
CHURCH HISTORY

HISTORIC CREEDS

Many Christians across the world affirm a creed of doctrinal beliefs. I encourage you to affirm regularly the earliest of these creedal confessions: the Apostles' Creed or the Nicene Creed. Note that we have not included "He descended into hell" because that expression was not in the earliest form of the Apostles' Creed.

APOSTLES'
CREED

I believe in God, the Father Almighty,
    Creator of heaven and earth.

I believe in Jesus Christ, His only Son, our Lord,
    who was conceived by the Holy Spirit
    and born of the virgin Mary.
    He suffered under Pontius Pilate,
    was crucified, died, and was buried;
    The third day He rose again from the dead.
    He ascended to heaven
    and is seated at the right hand of God
        the Father almighty.
    From there He will come to judge the living
        and the dead.

I believe in the Holy Spirit,
    the holy Christian church,
    the communion of saints,

the forgiveness of sins,
the resurrection of the body,
and the life everlasting. Amen.

NICENE CREED   We believe in one God,
the Father Almighty,
Maker of heaven and earth,
of all things visible and invisible.

And in one Lord Jesus Christ,
the only Son of God,
begotten from the Father before all ages,
God from God,
Light from Light,
true God from true God,
begotten, not made;
of the same essence as the Father.
Through Him all things were made.
For us and for our salvation
He came down from heaven;
He became incarnate by the Holy Spirit
and the virgin Mary,
and was made human.
He was crucified for us under Pontius Pilate;
He suffered and was buried.
The third day He rose again,
according to the Scriptures.
He ascended to heaven
and is seated at the right hand of the Father.

He will come again with glory
to judge the living and the dead.
His kingdom will never end.

And we believe in the Holy Spirit,
the Lord, the giver of life.
He proceeds from the Father and the Son,
and with the Father and the Son is worshiped
and glorified.
He spoke through the prophets.
We believe in one holy Christian
and apostolic church.

We affirm one baptism
for the forgiveness of sins.
We look forward to the resurrection of the dead,
and to life in the world to come. Amen.

TEN COMMANDMENTS

Ex 20:2-17 "I am Yahweh your God, who brought you out of the land of Egypt, out of the house of slavery.

I. You shall have no other gods before Me.

II. You shall not make for yourself an idol, or any likeness of what is in heaven above or on the earth beneath or in the water under the earth. You shall not worship them or serve them; for I, Yahweh your God, am a jealous God, visiting the iniquity of the fathers on the children, on the third and the fourth generations of those who hate Me, but showing lovingkindness to thousands, to those who love Me and keep My commandments.

III. You shall not take the name of Yahweh your God in vain, for Yahweh will not leave him unpunished who takes His name in vain.

IV. Remember the sabbath day, to keep it holy. Six days you shall labor and do all your work, but the seventh day is a sabbath of Yahweh your God; *in it* you shall not do any work, you or your son or your daughter, your male or your female slave or your cattle or your sojourner who is within your gates. For in six days Yahweh made the heavens and the earth, the sea and all that is in them, and rested on the seventh day; therefore Yahweh blessed the sabbath day and made it holy.

V. Honor your father and your mother, that your days may be prolonged in the land which Yahweh your God gives you.

VI. You shall not murder.

VII. You shall not commit adultery.

VIII. You shall not steal.

IX. You shall not bear false witness against your neighbor.

X. You shall not covet your neighbor's house; you shall not covet your neighbor's wife or his male slave or his female slave or his ox or his donkey or anything that belongs to your neighbor."

≫ FAVORITE PRAYERS ≪

Over the years I have gathered some favorite prayers that are not always composed directly of Scriptures, but express scriptural affirmations and requests. They are included here for your possible use.

GLORIA PATRI

Glory be to the Father
and to the Son and to the Holy Spirit.
As it was in the beginning,
is now and ever will be,
world without end. Amen.

DOXOLOGY

Praise God from whom all blessings flow.
Praise Him all creatures here below.
Praise Him above, you heavenly hosts.
Praise Father, Son, and Holy Ghost. Amen.

ORTHODOX PRAYER

Inflame my heart with love for You,
    O Christ my God,
that loving You with all my heart,
    with all my soul, with all my mind,
    and with all my strength,
and my neighbor as myself,
I may obey Your commands and glorify You,
    the Giver of all things.

"Heavenly Father, I worship you
    as the creator and sustainer of the universe.
Lord Jesus, I worship You,
    Savior and Lord of the world.
Holy Spirit, I worship You,
    sanctifier of the people of God.

Glory be to the Father, and to the Son,
    and to the Holy Spirit.

Heavenly Father, I pray that I may live
    this day in your presence and please you
    more and more.
Lord Jesus, I pray that this day I will take up
    my cross and follow you.
Holy Spirit, I pray that this day You will fill me
    with Yourself and cause Your fruit to ripen
    in my life: love, joy, peace, patience, kindness,
    goodness, faithfulness, gentleness and
    self-control.

Holy, blessed and glorious Trinity,
    three persons in one God,
    have mercy upon me, Amen."

PRAYER OF
GENERAL
THANKSGIVING

Book of
Common
Prayer

"Almighty God, Father of all mercies, we your unworthy servants do give you our most humble and hearty thanks for all your goodness and lovingkindness to us, and to all people. We bless you for our creation and preservation and for all the blessings of this life. But above all, we thank you for your inestimable love in the redemption of the world by our Lord Jesus Christ. We also thank you for the means of grace and for the hope of glory.

We beseech you now to give us that due sense of all your mercies, that our hearts may be truly thankful, and that we may show forth your praise, not only with our lips, but in our lives; by giving up ourselves to your service, and by walking before you in holiness and righteousness all our days; through Jesus Christ our Lord, to whom with you and the Holy Spirit be all honor and glory, world without end. Amen."

CONFESSION
OF SIN

Adapted
from the
*Book of
Common
Prayer*

Almighty and most merciful Father, I have erred and strayed from Your ways like a lost sheep. I have followed too much the devices and desires of my own heart. I have offended against Your holy laws. I have left undone those things which I ought to have done, and I have done those things which I ought not to have done; and apart from Your grace, there is no health in me.

O Lord, have mercy upon me. Spare all those who confess their faults. Restore all those who are penitent, according to Your promises declared to all people in Christ Jesus our Lord. And grant, O most merciful Father, for His sake, that I may now live a godly, righteous, and sober life, to the glory of Your holy Name. Amen.

Ps 5:1-3 Give ear to my words, O Yahweh,
Consider my meditation.
Give heed to the sound of my cry for help,
    my King and my God,
For to You I pray.
O Yahweh, in the morning,
You will hear my voice;
In the morning I will order *my prayer*
    to You and *eagerly* watch.

Ps 59:16 But as for me, I shall sing of Your strength;
And I shall joyfully sing of Your lovingkindness
    in the morning,
For You have been my stronghold
And a refuge in the day of my distress.

Ps 92:1-2 It is good to give thanks to Yahweh
And to sing praises to Your name, O Most High;
To declare Your lovingkindness in the morning
And Your faithfulness by night.

Adapted
from the
Book of
Common
Prayer

Lord God, Almighty and Everlasting Father,
You have brought me safely to this new day.
Preserve me with Your mighty power, that
I might not fall into sin or be overcome by
adversity. And in all I do direct me to fulfill
Your purpose by Your providence, through
Jesus Christ my Lord. Amen.

Lift up the light of Your face upon us,
O Yahweh!
You have put gladness in my heart,
More than when their grain
and new wine abound.
In peace I will both lie down and sleep,
For You alone, O Yahweh, make me
to abide in safety.

Luke 2:29-32

Now Master, You are releasing
Your slave in peace,
According to Your word.
For my eyes have seen Your salvation,
Which You prepared in the presence
of all peoples,
A LIGHT FOR REVELATION TO THE GENTILES,
And for the glory of Your people Israel.

Adapted
from the
Book of
Common
Prayer

Lighten my darkness, I beseech You, O Lord;
and by Your great mercy defend me from all
perils and dangers of this night. Keep watch,
dear Lord, over those who work, or watch, or
weep this night, and give Your angels charge
over those who sleep. Tend the sick, Lord Christ;
give rest to the weary, bless the dying, soothe
the suffering, pity the afflicted, and shield the
joyous. Guide me waking, O Lord, and guard me
sleeping; that awake I may watch with Christ,
and asleep I may rest in peace.

"LORD, HIGH AND HOLY, MEEK AND LOWLY,
Thou has brought me to the valley of vision,
where I live in the depths but see thee
    in the heights;
hemmed in by mountains of sin
    I behold thy glory.

Let me learn by paradox
    that the way down is the way up,
    that to be low is to be high,
    that the broken heart is the healed heart,
    that the contrite spirit is the rejoicing spirit,
    that the repenting soul is the victorious soul,
    that to have nothing is to possess all,
    that to bear the cross is to wear the crown,
    that to give is to receive,
    that the valley is the place of vision.

Lord, in the daytime stars can be seen
    from the deepest wells,
    and the deeper the wells
    the brighter thy stars shine;

Let me find thy light in my darkness,
    thy life in my death,
    thy joy in my sorrow,
    thy grace in my sin,
    thy riches in my poverty,
    thy glory in my valley."

APPENDIX TWO

—

PRAYERS FOR CHRISTIAN HOLIDAYS

There is a long-standing tradition to follow what has been called the "rhythms" of the Christian year. While the following Scriptures are not prayers, they are verses that are proper to prayerfully affirm during the special days when we observe the Passion, Ascension, and Advent of our Savior. I have also included Scripture for another special day to remember events that "reformed" the Gospel for us.

PASSION WEEK

PALM SUNDAY
Zech 9:9

Rejoice greatly, O daughter of Zion!
Make a loud shout, O daughter of Jerusalem!
Behold, your king is coming to you;
He is righteous and endowed with salvation,
Lowly and mounted on a donkey,
Even on a colt, the foal of a pack animal.

Matt 21:8-11

And most of the crowd spread their garments in the road, and others were cutting branches from the trees and spreading them in the road. And the crowds going ahead of Him, and those who followed, were crying out, saying, "Hosanna to the Son of David; BLESSED IS HE WHO COMES IN THE NAME OF THE LORD; Hosanna in the highest!" And when He had entered Jerusalem, all the city was stirred, saying, "Who is this?" And the crowds were saying, "This is the prophet Jesus, from Nazareth in Galilee."

The following Scriptures are coordinated with the six hours that Jesus was on the Cross, focusing on each of His seven sayings.

GOOD FRIDAY
9 A.M.
Luke 23:32-38

Now two others also, who were criminals, were being led away to be put to death with Him. And when they came to the place called The Skull, there they crucified Him and the criminals, one on the right and the other on the left. But Jesus was saying, "Father, forgive them; for they do not know what they are doing."AND THEY CAST LOTS, DIVIDING UP HIS GARMENTS AMONG THEMSELVES. And the people stood by, looking on. And even the rulers were scoffing at Him, saying, "He saved others; let Him save Himself if this is the Christ of God, His Chosen One." And the soldiers also mocked Him, coming up to Him, offering Him sour wine, and saying, "If You are the King of the Jews, save Yourself!" Now there was also an inscription above Him, "THIS IS THE KING OF THE JEWS."

10 A.M.
Luke 23:39-43

And one of the criminals hanging *there* was blaspheming Him, saying, "Are You not the Christ? Save Yourself and us!" But the other answered, and rebuking him said, "Do you not even fear God, since you are under the same sentence of condemnation? And we indeed *are suffering* justly, for we are receiving what we deserve for what we have done; but this man has done nothing wrong."

And he was saying, "Jesus, remember me when You come in Your kingdom!" And He said to him, "Truly I say to you, today you shall be with Me in Paradise."

11 A.M.
John 19:25-27

Therefore the soldiers did these things. But standing by the cross of Jesus were His mother, and His mother's sister, Mary the *wife* of Clopas, and Mary Magdalene. When Jesus then saw His mother, and the disciple whom He loved standing nearby, He said to His mother, "Woman, behold, your son!" Then He said to the disciple, "Behold, your mother!" From that hour the disciple took her into his *home.*

NOON
Matt 27:45-46

Now from the sixth hour darkness fell upon all the land until the ninth hour. And about the ninth hour Jesus cried out with a loud voice, saying, "ELI, ELI, LAMA SABACHTHANI?" that is, "MY GOD, MY GOD, WHY HAVE YOU FORSAKEN ME?"

1 P.M.
John 19:28-29

After this, Jesus, knowing that all things had already been finished, in order to finish the Scripture, said, "I am thirsty." A jar full of sour wine was standing there; so they put a sponge full of the sour wine upon *a branch of* hyssop and brought it up to His mouth.

2 P.M.
John 19:30

Therefore when Jesus had received the sour wine, He said, "It is finished!" And bowing His head, He gave up His spirit.

3 P.M.
Luke 23:44-46

And it was now about the sixth hour, and darkness fell over the whole land until the ninth hour, because the sun was obscured. And the veil of the sanctuary was torn in two. And Jesus, crying out with a loud voice, said, "Father, INTO YOUR HANDS I COMMIT MY SPIRIT." Having said this, He breathed His last.

RESURRECTION SUNDAY
Ps 16:8-11

I have set Yahweh continually before me;
Because He is at my right hand, I will not
    be shaken.
Therefore my heart is glad and my glory rejoices;
My flesh also will dwell securely.
For You will not forsake my soul to Sheol;
You will not give Your Holy One over to
    see corruption.
You will make known to me the path of life;
In Your presence is fullness of joy;
In Your right hand there are pleasures forever.

Matt 28:1-7

Now after the Sabbath, as it began to dawn toward the first *day* of the week, Mary Magdalene and the other Mary came to look at the grave. And behold, there was a great earthquake, for an angel of the Lord descended from heaven and came and rolled away the stone and sat upon it. And his appearance was like lightning, and his clothing as white as snow. And the guards quaked from fear of him and became like dead men. And the angel answered and said to the women, "Do not be afraid; for I know that you are looking for Jesus who has been crucified. He is not here, for He has risen, just as He said. Come, see the place where He was lying. And go quickly and tell His disciples that He has risen from the dead; and behold, He is going ahead of you into Galilee, there you will see Him; behold, I have told you."

1 Cor 15:20-23 But now Christ has been raised from the dead, the first fruits of those who have fallen asleep. For since by a man *came* death, by a man also *came* the resurrection of the dead. For as in Adam all die, so also in Christ all will be made alive. But each in his own order: Christ the first fruits, after that those who are Christ's at His coming.

ASCENSION DAY

Acts 1:6-11 So when they had come together, they were asking Him, saying, "Lord, is it at this time You are restoring the kingdom to Israel?" But He said to them,
"It is not for you to know times or seasons
which the Father has set by His own authority;
but you will receive power when the Holy Spirit
has come upon you; and you shall be My witnesses
both in Jerusalem, and in all Judea and Samaria, and
even to THE END OF THE EARTH." And after
He had said these things, He was lifted up while
they were looking on, and a cloud received Him
out of their sight. And as they were gazing intently
into the sky while He was going, behold, two men in
white clothing stood beside them. They also said,
"Men of Galilee, why do you stand looking toward
heaven? This Jesus, who has been taken up from you
into heaven, will come in just the same way as you
have watched Him go into heaven."

PENTECOST SUNDAY

Acts 2:1-4   And when the day of Pentecost had fully
come, they were all together in one place.
And suddenly there came from heaven
a noise like a violent rushing wind, and
it filled the whole house where they
were sitting. And there appeared to them
tongues like fire distributing themselves,
and they rested on each one of them.
And they were all filled with the Holy Spirit
and began to speak with other tongues,
as the Spirit was giving them utterance.

Acts 2:32-36   This Jesus God raised up again, to which
we are all witnesses. Therefore having been
exalted to the right hand of God, and having
received from the Father the promise of the
Holy Spirit, He has poured out this which you
both see and hear. For David did not ascend
into the heavens, but he himself says:
   "The Lord said to my Lord,
   'Sit at My right hand,
   Until I put Your enemies
      as a footstool for Your feet.'"
Therefore let all the house of Israel know
for certain that God has made Him both Lord
and Christ—this Jesus whom you crucified.

REFORMATION DAY

Hab 2:3-4 Then Yahweh answered me and said,
    "Write down the vision
    And write *it* on tablets distinctly,
    That the one who reads it may run.
    For the vision is yet for the appointed time;
    It pants toward its end, and it will not lie.
    Though it tarries, wait for it;
    For it will certainly come; it will not delay.
    Behold, as for the proud one,
    His soul is not right within him;
    But the righteous will live by his faith."

Rom 1:16-17 For I am not ashamed of the gospel, for it is the power of God for salvation to everyone who believes, to the Jew first and also to the Greek. For in it *the* righteousness of God is revealed from faith to faith; as it is written, "BUT THE RIGHTEOUS WILL LIVE BY FAITH."

FIRST Then a shoot will spring from the stem of Jesse,
SUNDAY OF And a branch from his roots will bear fruit.
ADVENT The Spirit of Yahweh will rest on Him,
Is 11:1-2, 5 The spirit of wisdom and understanding,
The spirit of counsel and might,
The spirit of knowledge and the fear
of Yahweh.
Also righteousness will be the belt
about His loins,
And faithfulness the belt about His waist.

Jer 33:14-15 "Behold, days are coming," declares Yahweh,
"when I will establish the good word which
I have spoken concerning the house of Israel
and the house of Judah. In those days and
at that time I will cause a righteous Branch
of David to branch forth; and He shall do
justice and righteousness on the earth."

SECOND A voice is calling,
SUNDAY OF "Prepare the way for Yahweh in the wilderness;
ADVENT Make smooth in the desert a highway
Is 40:3-5 for our God.
Let every valley be lifted up,
And every mountain and hill be made low;
And let the rough ground become a plain,

And the rugged terrain a broad valley;
Then the glory of Yahweh will be revealed,
And all flesh will see it together;
For the mouth of Yahweh has spoken."

Is 40:9-11 Get yourself up on a high mountain,
O Zion, bearer of good news,
Raise up your voice powerfully,
O Jerusalem, bearer of good news;
Raise *it* up, do not fear.
Say to the cities of Judah,
"Behold your God!"
Behold, Lord Yahweh will come with strength,
With His arm ruling for Him.
Behold, His reward is with Him
And His recompense before Him.
Like a shepherd He will shepherd His flock;
In His arm He will gather the lambs
And carry *them* in His bosom;
He will gently lead the nursing *ewes*.

THIRD
SUNDAY OF
ADVENT
Mal 3:1; 4:5-6

"Behold, I am going to send My messenger,
and he will prepare the way before Me.
And the Lord, whom you seek, will suddenly
come to His temple; and the messenger of the
covenant, in whom you delight, behold, He is
coming," says Yahweh of hosts. "Behold, I am
going to send you Elijah the prophet before
the coming of the great and awesome day

of Yahweh. And he will turn the hearts of the
fathers to *their* children and the hearts of the
children to their fathers, lest I come and strike
the land, devoting it to destruction."

Zech 6:12-13 Then you will say to him, "Thus says Yahweh
of hosts, 'Behold, a man whose name is Branch,
and He will branch out from where He is; and
He will build the temple of Yahweh. Indeed,
it is He who will build the temple of Yahweh,
and He who will bear the splendor and sit
and rule on His throne. Thus, He will be a priest
on His throne, and the counsel of peace will be
between the two offices.'"

FOURTH   For a child will be born to us,
SUNDAY OF   a son will be given to us;
ADVENT   And the government will rest on His shoulders;
Is 9:6   And His name will be called
                Wonderful Counselor, Mighty God,
            Eternal Father, Prince of Peace.

Matt 1:18-23 Now the birth of Jesus Christ was as follows:
when His mother Mary had been betrothed
to Joseph, before they came together she was
found to be with child by the Holy Spirit.
And Joseph her husband, being a righteous man
and not wanting to disgrace her, planned
to send her away secretly. But when he had

considered this, behold, an angel of the Lord appeared to him in a dream, saying, "Joseph, son of David, do not be afraid to take Mary as your wife; for the One who has been conceived in her is of the Holy Spirit. And she will bear a Son; and you shall call His name Jesus, for He will save His people from their sins." Now all this took place in order that what was spoken by the Lord through the prophet would be fulfilled, saying, "BEHOLD, THE VIRGIN SHALL BE WITH CHILD AND SHALL BEAR A SON, AND THEY SHALL CALL HIS NAME IMMANUEL," which translated means, "GOD WITH US."

CHRISTMAS DAY
John 3:16-17

For God so loved the world, that He gave His only begotten Son, that whoever believes in Him shall not perish, but have eternal life. For God did not send the Son into the world to judge the world, but that the world might be saved through Him.

Titus 2:11-14

For the grace of God has appeared, bringing salvation to all men, instructing us that, denying ungodliness and worldly desires, we should live sensibly, righteously, and godly in the present age, looking for the blessed hope and the appearing of the glory of our great God and Savior, Jesus Christ, who gave Himself for us that He might redeem us from all lawlessness, and purify for Himself a people for His own possession, zealous for good works.

>>>>>><<<<<<

APPENDIX THREE

THREE

—

PRAYERS FOR THE CHRISTIAN LIFE

>>>>>><<<<<<

As we pray the Scriptures, those same Scriptures can also provide us with comfort and answers to questions on many topics! The topics listed below have a selection of Scriptures to guide your prayers. They can also easily be turned into your personal prayers.

ABOUT PRAYER 221

CHURCH 222

CONFLICT 223

DEATH 224

ENCOURAGEMENT 225

EVANGELISM 226

FAMILY 227

FEAR 228

FORGIVENESS 229

GOVERNMENT 230

GRIEF 231

GUIDANCE 232

HEALTH 233

HOPE 234

MARRIAGE 235

MOTIVATION 236

PROTECTION 237

PROVISION 238

REST 239

SPIRITUAL WARFARE . . 240

STRENGTH 241

TEMPTATION 242

THANKSGIVING 243

WAITING ON GOD 244

→ ABOUT PRAYER ←

2 Chr 7:14 If My people who are called by My name humble themselves and pray and seek My face and turn from their evil ways, then I will listen from heaven, I will forgive their sin, and I will heal their land.

Ps 66:19-20 But certainly God has heard;
He has given heed to the voice of my prayer.
Blessed be God,
Who has not turned away my prayer
Nor His lovingkindness from me.

Ps 102:17 He has turned toward the prayer of the destitute
And has not despised their prayer.

Matt 7:7-8 Ask, and it will be given to you; seek, and you will find; knock, and it will be opened to you. For everyone who asks receives, and he who seeks finds, and to him who knocks it will be opened.

James 5:16b The effective prayer of a righteous man can accomplish much.

ADDITIONAL
SCRIPTURE   *1 Kin 8:28 / Neh 1:11 / Ps 42:8 / Rev 5:8; 8:3-4*

→ CHURCH ←

*Acts 2:42 May I continually devote myself to the apostles'
teaching and to the fellowship, to the breaking
of bread and to the prayers.

1 Cor 12:18- But now God has appointed the members,
20 each one of them, in the body, just as He desired.
And if they were all one member, where would
the body be? But now there are many members,
but one body.

*Heb 10:25 I will not forsake our assembling together,
as is the habit of some, but I will encourage
other believers, and all the more as I see the
day drawing near.

*Heb 13:7 I remember my leaders, who spoke the word
of God to me; and considering the result
of their conduct, may I imitate their faith.

_____

ADDITIONAL *Ps 26:8-12 / 1 Cor 12:21-31*
SCRIPTURE

→ CONFLICT ←

Matt 5:38-39 You have heard that it was said, "AN EYE FOR AN EYE, AND A TOOTH FOR A TOOTH." But I say to you, do not resist an evil person; but whoever slaps you on your right cheek, turn the other to him also.

Matt 18:15-17 Now if your brother sins, go and show him his fault, between you and him alone; if he listens to you, you have won your brother. But if he does not listen *to you*, take one or two more with you, so that BY THE MOUTH OF TWO OR THREE WITNESSES EVERY FACT MAY BE CONFIRMED. And if he refuses to listen to them, tell it to the church; and if he refuses to listen even to the church, let him be to you as the Gentile and the tax collector.

Rom 12:17-19 Never paying back evil for evil to anyone, respecting what is good in the sight of all men, if possible, so far as it depends on you, being at peace with all men, never taking your own revenge, beloved—instead leave room for the wrath *of God*. For it is written, "VENGEANCE IS MINE, I WILL REPAY," says the Lord.

ADDITIONAL SCRIPTURE *Lev 19:18 / Prov 15:1; 16:7 / Matt 5:9, 24, 40-42; 7:5 / John 13:34-35 / 1 Cor 13:4-7 / Gal 6:1 / Eph 4:25-29 / Phil 2:2-4 / Col 3:13 / 1 Pet 3:8-11*

⇝ DEATH ⇜

Job 1:21   And he said,

      "Naked I came from my mother's womb,
       And naked I shall return there.
       Yahweh gave, and Yahweh has taken away.
       Blessed be the name of Yahweh."

Job 19:25-27   As for me, I know that my Redeemer lives,
     And at the last He will rise up over the dust
       of this world.
     Even after my skin is destroyed,
     Yet from my flesh I shall behold God,
     Whom I myself shall behold,
     And whom my eyes will see and not another.
     My heart faints within me!

Phil 1:21-24   For to me, to live is Christ and to die is gain.
But if *I am* to live *on* in the flesh, this *will mean*
fruitful labor for me; and I do not know what I
will choose. But I am hard-pressed between the two,
having the desire to depart and be with Christ,
for *that* is very much better, yet to remain on
in the flesh is more necessary for your sake.

ADDITIONAL   *Job 2:10 / 2 Cor 5:1-8 / 1 Thess 4:13-18 / Rev 14:13*
SCRIPTURE

⇢ ENCOURAGEMENT ⇠

Ps 37:23-24 The footsteps of a man are established
　　　by Yahweh,
And He delights in his way.
When he falls, he will not be hurled headlong,
Because Yahweh is the One
　　　who sustains his hand.

Phil 1:6 *For I am* confident of this very thing, that He
who began a good work in you will perfect it
until the day of Christ Jesus.

Phil 4:7 And the peace of God, which surpasses all
comprehension, will guard your hearts and
your minds in Christ Jesus.

Heb 10:24-25 And let us consider how to stimulate one another
to love and good deeds, not forsaking our own
assembling together, as is the habit of some,
but encouraging *one another*, and all the more
as you see the day drawing near.

ADDITIONAL
SCRIPTURE

2 Cor 5:6-7 / 1 Thess 2:11-12 / 1 John 4:4

→ EVANGELISM ←

Matt 28:19-20 Go therefore and make disciples of all the nations,
baptizing them in the name of the Father
and the Son and the Holy Spirit, teaching them
to keep all that I commanded you; and behold,
I am with you always, even to the end of the age.

Rom 1:16 For I am not ashamed of the gospel, for it is
the power of God for salvation to everyone
who believes, to the Jew first and also to the Greek.

1 Cor 1:17 For Christ did not send me to baptize, but to
proclaim the gospel, not in wisdom of word,
so that the cross of Christ will not be made empty.

2 Cor 5:20 So then, we are ambassadors for Christ, as God
is pleading through us. We beg you on behalf of
Christ, be reconciled to God.

1 Pet 3:15 But sanctify Christ as Lord in your hearts, always
being ready to make a defense to everyone who asks
you to give an account for the hope that is in you,
yet with gentleness and fear.

ADDITIONAL SCRIPTURE *Matt 9:37-38 / Acts 20:21 / 2 Tim 4:5*

⇒ FAMILY ⇐

Ps 127:3-5   Behold, children are an inheritance of Yahweh,
            The fruit of the womb is a reward.
            Like arrows in the hand of a warrior,
            So are the children of one's youth.
            How blessed is the man who fills his quiver
                with them;
            They will not be ashamed
            When they speak with enemies in the gate.

Prov 22:6   Train up a child according to his way,
            Even when he is old he will not depart from it.

Eph 6:4   Fathers, do not provoke your children
            to anger, but bring them up in the discipline
            and instruction of the Lord.

Col 3:20-21 Children, obey your parents in all things, for this
            is pleasing to the Lord. Fathers, do not exasperate
            your children, so that they will not lose heart.

1 Tim 5:8   But if anyone does not provide for his own, and
            especially for those of his household, he has
            denied the faith and is worse than an unbeliever.

ADDITIONAL   *Ex 20:12 / Prov 6:20 / 1 Tim 3:4-5*
SCRIPTURE

→ FEAR ←

Ps 55:4-6,
16-17, 22

My heart is in anguish within me,
And the terrors of death have fallen upon me.
Fear and trembling come upon me,
And horror has covered me.
I said, "Oh, that I had wings like a dove!
I would fly away and be at rest."
As for me, I shall call upon God,
And Yahweh will save me.
Evening and morning and at noon,
I will bring my complaint and moan,
And He will hear my voice.
I will cast my burden upon Yahweh
    and He will sustain me;
He will never allow the righteous to be shaken.

Rev 2:9-10

I know your tribulation and your poverty (but you
are rich), and the blasphemy by those who say they
are Jews and are not, but are a synagogue of Satan.
Do not fear what you are about to suffer. Behold,
the devil is about to cast some of you into prison,
so that you will be tested, and you will have
tribulation for ten days. Be faithful until death,
and I will give you the crown of life.

ADDITIONAL   *Ps 56:3-13*
SCRIPTURE

⇢ FORGIVENESS ⇠

Ps 103:12 As far as the east is from the west,
So far has He removed our transgressions
from us.

Is 1:18 "Come now, and let us reason together,"
Says Yahweh,
"Though your sins are as scarlet,
They will be as white as snow;
Though they are red like crimson,
They will be like wool."

Is 43:25 I, even I, am the one who wipes out your
transgressions for My own sake,
And I will not remember your sins.

Eph 1:7 In Him we have redemption through His blood,
the forgiveness of our transgressions, according
to the riches of God's grace.

1 John 1:8-9 If we say that we have no sin, we deceive
ourselves and the truth is not in us. If we
confess our sins, He is faithful and righteous
to forgive us our sins and to cleanse us from
all unrighteousness.

ADDITIONAL SCRIPTURE *Mark 11:24-25 / 1 John 1:9-2:2*

⇒ GOVERNMENT ⇐

Matt 22:21b   Therefore, render to Caesar the things that are Caesar's; and to God the things that are God's.

Acts 5:29b   We must obey God rather than men.

Titus 3:1   Remind them to be subject to rulers, to authorities, to be obedient, to be ready for every good work.

1 Pet 2:13-15   Be subject for the sake of the Lord to every human institution, whether to a king as the one in authority, or to governors as sent by him for the punishment of evildoers and the praise of those who do good. For such is the will of God that by doing good you may silence the ignorance of foolish men.

ADDITIONAL SCRIPTURE   *Matt 22:17-21 / Acts 5:28-29 / Rom 13:1-7*

⇢ GRIEF ⇠

Ps 119:28 My soul weeps because of grief;
Raise me up according to Your word.

John 14:1-6 "Do not let your heart be troubled; believe
in God, believe also in Me. In My Father's house
are many dwelling places; if it were not so,
I would have told you; for I go to prepare a place
for you. And if I go and prepare a place for you,
I will come again and receive you to Myself,
that where I am, *there* you may be also. And you
know the way where I am going." Thomas said
to Him, "Lord, we do not know where You
are going. How do we know the way?" Jesus said
to him, "I am the way, and the truth, and the life.
No one comes to the Father but through Me."

2 Cor 1:3-4 Blessed *be* the God and Father of our Lord Jesus
Christ, the Father of mercies and God of all
comfort, who comforts us in all our affliction
so that we will be able to comfort those who are
in any affliction with the comfort with which
we ourselves are comforted by God.

ADDITIONAL   *Is 53:3-4, 10 / Lam 3:32*
SCRIPTURE

→ GUIDANCE ←

Ex 15:13 In Your lovingkindness You have guided
      the people whom You have redeemed;
In Your strength You have led *them*
      to Your holy habitation.

Ps 23:1-2 Yahweh is my shepherd,
I shall not want.
He makes me lie down in green pastures;
He leads me beside quiet waters.

Prov 1:5 Let the wise man hear and increase in learning,
And a man of understanding will acquire guidance.

1 Tim 6:17-19 Command those who are rich in this present age
not to be haughty or to set their hope on the
uncertainty of riches, but on God, who richly
supplies us with all things to enjoy. *Command
them* to do good, to be rich in good works,
to be generous and ready to share, storing up
for themselves the treasure of a good foundation
for the future, so that they may take hold of that
which is life indeed.

➔ HEALTH ←

1 Cor 6:19-20 Or do you not know that your body is
a sanctuary of the Holy Spirit who is in you,
whom you have from God, and that you are not
your own? For you were bought with a price:
therefore glorify God in your body.

James 5:13-15 Is anyone among you suffering? *Then* he must
pray. Is anyone cheerful? He is to sing praises.
Is anyone among you sick? *Then* he must call
for the elders of the church and they are to pray
over him, anointing him with oil in the name
of the Lord. And the prayer offered in faith
will save the one who is sick, and the Lord
will raise him up, and if he has committed sins,
they will be forgiven him.

3 John 2 Beloved, I pray that in all respects you may
prosper and be in good health, just as your
soul prospers.

ADDITIONAL   *Ex 23:25 / Ps 147:3 / Prov 3:7-8; 16:24 / 1 Tim 4:8*
SCRIPTURE

→ HOPE ←

Lam 3:21-25   This I will return to my heart;
Therefore I will wait in hope.
The lovingkindnesses of Yahweh
   indeed never cease,
For His compassions never fail.
They are new every morning;
Great is Your faithfulness.
"Yahweh is my portion," says my soul,
"Therefore I wait for Him."
Yahweh is good to those who hope in Him,
To the soul who seeks Him.

Rom 15:13   Now may the God of hope fill you with all joy
and peace in believing, so that you will abound
in hope by the power of the Holy Spirit.

Heb 6:19-20   This hope we have as an anchor of the soul, a *hope*
both sure and confirmed and one which enters
within the veil, where a forerunner has entered
for us—Jesus, having become a high priest forever
according to the order of Melchizedek.

Heb 10:23   Let us hold fast the confession of our hope
without wavering, for He who promised is faithful.

ADDITIONAL   *Ps 62:5-8 / Is 26:7-9 / Rom 15:4 / Heb 11:1*
SCRIPTURE

⇢ MARRIAGE ⇠

Song 8:6-7 Put me like a seal over your heart,
Like a seal on your arm.
For love is as strong as death,
Jealousy is as severe as Sheol;
Its flashes are flashes of fire,
The *very* flame of Yah.
Many waters cannot quench love,
Nor will rivers overflow it;
If a man were to give all the riches
of his house for love,
It would be utterly despised.

Mark 10:6-9 But from the beginning of creation, *God* MADE
THEM MALE AND FEMALE. FOR THIS REASON A MAN
SHALL LEAVE HIS FATHER AND MOTHER, AND THE
TWO SHALL BECOME ONE FLESH; so they are
no longer two, but one flesh. What therefore
God has joined together, let no man separate.

Col 3:18-19 Wives, be subject to your husbands, as is fitting
in the Lord. Husbands, love your wives
and do not be embittered against them.

ADDITIONAL
SCRIPTURE
Eph 5:22-33 / 1 Pet 3:1-7

→ MOTIVATION ←

Ezra 10:4   Arise! For *this* matter is your responsibility, but we will be with you; be strong and act.

John 16:33   These things I have spoken to you, so that in Me you may have peace. In the world you have tribulation, but take courage; I have overcome the world.

Rom 12:2   And do not be conformed to this world, but be transformed by the renewing of your mind, so that you may approve what the will of God is, that which is good and pleasing and perfect.

Phil 3:13-14   Brothers, I do not consider myself as having laid hold of *it* yet, but one thing *I do*: forgetting what *lies* behind and reaching forward to what *lies* ahead, I press on toward the goal for the prize of the upward call of God in Christ Jesus.

⇒ PROTECTION ⇐

Deut 31:6   Be strong and courageous. Do not be afraid
or be in dread of them, for Yahweh your God
is the one who goes with you. He will not fail
you or forsake you.

Ps 32:7   You are my hiding place;
    You guard me from trouble;
You surround me with songs
    of deliverance.   Selah.

Is 43:2   When you pass through the waters,
    I will be with you;
And through the rivers, they will not
    overflow you.
When you walk through the fire,
    you will not be scorched,
Nor will the flame burn you.

2 Thess 3:1-3   Finally, brothers, pray for us that the word
of the Lord will spread rapidly and be glorified,
just as *it did* also with you; and that we will be
rescued from perverse and evil men, for not all
have faith. But the Lord is faithful, who will
strengthen and guard you from the evil one.

ADDITIONAL   *Ps 16:8; 34:19 / Is 54:17*
SCRIPTURE

➔ PROVISION ➔

Ps 34:10 The young lions do lack and suffer hunger;
But they who inquire of Yahweh shall not be
in want of any good thing.

Matt 6:31-33 Do not worry then, saying, "What will we eat?"
or "What will we drink?" or "What will we wear
for clothing?" For all these things the Gentiles
eagerly seek; for your heavenly Father knows
that you need all these things. But seek first His
kingdom and His righteousness, and all these
things will be added to you.

Matt 7:11 If you then, being evil, know how to give good gifts
to your children, how much more will your
Father who is in heaven give what is good to those
who ask Him!

Luke 12:22-24 And He said to His disciples, "For this reason I say
to you, do not worry about *your* life, *as to* what
you will eat; nor for your body, *as to* what you will
put on. For life is more than food, and the body
more than clothing. Consider the ravens, for they
neither sow nor reap; they have no storeroom nor
barn, and *yet* God feeds them; how much more
valuable you are than the birds!"

ADDITIONAL SCRIPTURE *2 Cor 9:8-11 / Phil 4:19*

➤ REST ⬅

Gen 2:2-3 And on the seventh day God completed His work which He had done, and He rested on the seventh day from all His work which He had done. Then God blessed the seventh day and sanctified it, because on it He rested from all His work which God had created in making *it*.

Ex 20:11 For in six days Yahweh made the heavens and the earth, the sea and all that is in them, and rested on the seventh day; therefore Yahweh blessed the sabbath day and made it holy.

Ps 116:7 Return to your rest, O my soul,
For Yahweh has dealt bountifully with you.

Jer 6:16a Thus says Yahweh,
"Stand by the ways and see and ask
for the ancient paths,
Where the good way is, and walk in it;
And you will find rest for your souls."

Matt 11:28-29 Come to Me, all who are weary and heavy-laden, and I will give you rest. Take My yoke upon you and learn from Me, for I am gentle and humble in heart, and YOU WILL FIND REST FOR YOUR SOULS.

ADDITIONAL SCRIPTURE *Ex 23:11-12 / Deut 12:10 / Ps 55:6; 62:7 / Is 30:15 / Mark 6:31 / 2 Thess 1:6-8 / Heb 4:1-3; 4:8-11*

2 Cor 10:3-5 For though we walk in the flesh, we do not war according to the flesh, for the weapons of our warfare are not of the flesh, but divinely powerful for the tearing down of strongholds, as we tear down speculations and every lofty thing raised up against the knowledge of God, and take every thought captive to the obedience of Christ.

Eph 6:13-17 Therefore, take up the full armor of God, so that you will be able to resist in the evil day, and having done everything, to stand firm. Stand firm therefore, HAVING GIRDED YOUR LOINS WITH TRUTH, and HAVING PUT ON THE BREASTPLATE OF RIGHTEOUSNESS, and having shod YOUR FEET WITH THE PREPARATION OF THE GOSPEL OF PEACE. in addition to all, having taken up the shield of faith with which you will be able to extinguish all the flaming arrows of the evil one, also receive THE HELMET OF SALVATION, and the sword of the Spirit, which is the word of God.

James 4:7-8a Be subject therefore to God. Resist the devil and he will flee from you. Draw near to God and He will draw near to you.

ADDITIONAL   *John 16:33 / Rom 8:37-39 / Eph 6:10-11 / 2 Thess 3:3 /*
SCRIPTURE   *1 Pet 5:8-9*

➔ STRENGTH ←

Deut 31:6   Be strong and courageous. Do not be afraid or be in dread of them, for Yahweh your God is the one who goes with you. He will not fail you or forsake you.

Ps 118:14   Yah is my strength and song,
And He has become my salvation.

Phil 4:12-13   I know how to get along with humble means, and I also know how to live in abundance; in any and all things I have learned the secret of being filled and going hungry, both of having abundance and suffering need. I can do all things through Him who strengthens me.

Heb 12:1-3   Therefore, since we have so great a cloud of witnesses surrounding us, laying aside every weight and the sin which so easily entangles us, let us run with endurance the race that is set before us, fixing our eyes on Jesus, the author and perfecter of faith, who for the joy set before Him endured the cross, despising the shame, and has sat down at the right hand of the throne of God. For consider Him who has endured such hostility by sinners against Himself, so that you will not grow weary, fainting in heart.

**ADDITIONAL
SCRIPTURE**   *Ps 28:6-7; 31:1-5*

→ TEMPTATION ←

1 Cor 10:13 No temptation has overtaken you but such as is common to man, but God is faithful, who will not allow you to be tempted beyond what you are able, but with the temptation will provide the way of escape also, so that you will be able to endure it.

James 1:12 Blessed is a man who perseveres under trial; for once he has been approved, he will receive the crown of life which *the Lord* has promised to those who love Him.

1 John 1:9-2:2 If we confess our sins, He is faithful and righteous to forgive us our sins and to cleanse us from all unrighteousness. If we say that we have not sinned, we make Him a liar and His word is not in us. My little children, I am writing these things to you so that you may not sin. And if anyone sins, we have an Advocate with the Father, Jesus Christ the righteous; and He Himself is the propitiation for our sins, and not for ours only, but also for *those of* the whole world.

ADDITIONAL SCRIPTURE *Matt 6:13; 26:41*

→ THANKSGIVING ←

Is 12:4-5　And in that day you will say,
　　　　"Give thanks to Yahweh, call on His name.
　　　　Make known His deeds among the peoples;
　　　　Make *them* remember that His name is exalted."
　　　　Praise Yahweh in song,
　　　　　　for He has done majestic things;
　　　　Let this be known throughout the earth.

2 Cor 2:14　But thanks be to God, who always leads us in
　　　　triumphal procession in Christ, and manifests
　　　　through us the aroma of the knowledge
　　　　of Him in every place.

1 Thess 5:18　In everything give thanks, for this is God's will
　　　　for you in Christ Jesus.

1 Tim 4:4　For everything created by God is good,
　　　　and nothing is to be rejected if it is received
　　　　with thanksgiving.

ADDITIONAL　*Ps 95:1-7*
SCRIPTURE

Ex 14:13b, 14 Do not fear! Stand by and see the salvation
of Yahweh which He will accomplish
for you today. Yahweh will fight for you,
and you will keep silent.

Is 30:18 Therefore Yahweh waits *with longing*
to be gracious to you,
And therefore He is on high
to have compassion on you.
For Yahweh is a God of justice;
How blessed are all those who wait for Him.

Rom 8:24-25 For in hope we were saved, but hope that is seen
is not hope, for who hopes for what he *already* sees?
But if we hope for what we do not see,
with perseverance we eagerly wait for it.

2 Pet 3:8-9 But do not let this one *fact* escape your notice,
beloved, that with the Lord one day is like a
thousand years, and a thousand years like one
day. The Lord is not slow about His promise,
as some consider slowness, but is patient
toward you, not willing for any to perish but
for all to come to repentance.

ADDITIONAL   *Ps 27:13-14; 130:5-7*
SCRIPTURE

EPILOGUE

I end this book by affirming the following about the God to whom we pray:

> Yahweh is my God, Yahweh is one!
> I will love Yahweh my God with all my
> heart and with all my soul and with
> all my might. (*Deut 6:4-5*)

> The Rock! His work is perfect,
> For all His ways are just;
> A God of faithfulness and without injustice,
> Righteous and upright is He. (*Deut 32:4*)

> Oh, the depth of the riches and the
> wisdom of knowing You, O God! How
> unsearchable are Your judgments and
> unfathomable Your ways! For who has
> known Your mind, O Lord, or who has
> become Your counselor? For from You
> and through You and to You are all things.
> To You be the glory forever. Amen.
> (*Rom 11:33-36*)

SCRIPTURE INDEX

GENESIS

2:2-3	239

EXODUS

3:13-15	10
14:13b, 14	244
15:13	232
20:2-17	192
20:11	239
20:12	227
23:11-12	239
23:25	233

LEVITICUS

19:18	223

NUMBERS

6:24-26	28, 44, 64, 88, 112, 120, 137, 157, 183

DEUTERONOMY

6:4-5	18, 181, 247
12:10	239
31:6	237, 241
32:4	247

1 SAMUEL

2:2	114
2:2, 8	70
2:9-10	74, 107, 139

2 SAMUEL

22:2b-4	153

1 KINGS

8:28	221
8:56-60	162
8:56a, 58, 60	32

1 CHRONICLES

16:34	17
29:11-13, 18	60
29:18	137

2 CHRONICLES

6:29-31a	24
6:30-31	68, 124
7:13-14	94
7:14	221

EZRA

9:6, 8	58, 130
10:4	236

NEHEMIAH

1:11	221

JOB

1:21	12, 224
2:10	224
9:9-10	56, 129
14:14	47
19:25-26	66, 118

JOB (CONTINUED)

19:25-27	224

PSALMS

1:1-3	54, 102
1:1a, 2-3	160
3:8	44, 115, 134, 167, 178
4:1, 4-5	29
4:6b-8	199
4:7-8	154
5:1-3	51, 85, 198
5:11-12	57, 105
8:1-4	105
10:17-18	90
12:6-7	131
16:1-6	166
16:1-3, 5-6	35
16:8	237
16:8-11	208
18:6	86, 181
18:30-32	50, 110, 176
19:12-13	54, 113
19:14	Daily
23:1-2	232
25:6-11	25, 50, 106, 122, 154, 180
25:8-11, 16-18	77
25:10-11	18
25:20-21	39, 171
26:8-12	222
27:1-4	112
27:4	91
27:7-8	63, 119, 161
27:13-14	244
28:6-7	241
31:1-5	39, 136, 171, 241
32:1-5	22, 164
32:3-5	66, 126, 175
32:7	237
34:1-3	17, 81
34:6-7	41, 117, 164
34:10	238
34:18-20	86, 98
34:19	237
36:5-9	121
37:23-24	225
37:39-40	65, 126
40:1-3	37, 134, 163
42:1-2	101
42:1-5	174
42:1-2, 5	37
42:8	221
44:4-8	80, 96, 103
51:1-3	85, 139
51:1-10, 12-13	148
51:10-15	169
55:4-6, 16-17, 22	228
55:6	239
55:16-17	26, 122, 181

55:16-17, 22	30, 62	*116:7*	239
56:3-13	228	*118:14*	241
57:9-11	68, 125	*118:25-27a, 28-29*	21
59:16	198	*119:28*	231
62:1-2	148	*119:97*	34, 102, 160
62:5-8	234	*119:162-168*	22
62:7	239	*119:164-168*	69, 89
63:1-3	134	*121*	99
63:1-4	41	*121:1-3*	55, 83
63:1-5	158	*121:1-4*	113
63:4b-8	179	*124*	88
66:19-20	221	*127:3-5*	227
72:17-19	152	*130:5-7*	244
72:18-19	36, 141, 173	*135:5-6*	96
85:4-7	20	*135:13*	96
86:11-12	63, 91, 182	*135:13, 20b-21*	52
89:1-2	25, 138, 158	*135:13, 21*	133
92:1-2	69, 113, 198	*139:1-6*	49, 163
94:22	17, 101	*139:7-12*	53, 168
95:1-7	243	*139:13-16*	57
96:1-6	147	*139:13-18*	168
100	89, 179	*139:17-18*	61
102:17	221	*139:23-24*	Daily
103:1-5	174	*143:7-9*	87, 177
103:12	229	*147:3*	233
103:19-22	45	*148:1-5*	93, 117
103:20-22	29, 73, 126	*150*	65, 138, 153
107:8-9	53, 109, 130, 158	*150:1-2, 6*	33
111:1-6	93		

PROVERBS

1:5	232
3:7-8	233
6:20	227
15:1	223
16:7	223
16:24	233
22:6	227

ECCLESIASTES

7:20	73, 101

SONG OF SONGS

8:6-7	235

ISAIAH

1:18	69, 81, 229
9:6	215
11:1-2, 5	213
12:1-5	142
12:4-5	49, 243
26:7-9	234
30:15	239
30:18	244
40:3-5	213
40:9-11	214
42:6-7	172
43:2	237
43:25	229
53:3-4, 10	231
54:17	237
55:11	18
57:15	30 ,114, 176

58:6-9a	151
61:10-11	148
64:6-7a, 8	52

JEREMIAH

6:16a	239
15:16	13
17:9-10	61, 135
31:3	33
33:14-15	213

LAMENTATIONS

3:21-25	234
3:32	231

DANIEL

4:34b-35	42
9:7, 17	33, 159

AMOS

4:13	25, 130

JONAH

4:2b	46, 118, 159

HABAKKUK

2:3-4	212
2:4	94, 165
3:17-19a	46, 127, 165

ZECHARIAH

6:12-13	215
9:9	205

MALACHI

1:11	66, 118
3:1; 4:5-6	214

MATTHEW

1:18-23	215
5:9	223
5:24	223
5:38-39	223
5:40-42	223
5:44-45	80, 104
6:9-13	8
6:9b-13	Daily
6:13	242
6:19-21	150
6:31-33	238
7:5	223
7:7-8	221
7:11	238
9:37-38	63, 226
9:37b-38	129, 157, 182
11:28-29	239
18:15-27	223
21:8-11	205
22:17-21	230
22:21b	230
26:41	242
27:45-46	207
28:1-7	208
28:19-20	226

MARK

6:31	239
10:6-9	235
11:24-25	229

LUKE

2:29-32	199
12:22-24	238
15:7, 10b	61, 121
23:32-38	206
23:39-43	206
23:44-46	208

JOHN

3:16-17	216
4:23-24	110
4:24	170
4:35	129
13:34-35	223
15:7-11	103
16:33	236, 240
17	8
19:25-27	207
19:28-29	207
19:30	208

ACTS

1:6-11	210
2:1-4	211
2:32-36	211
2:42	222
5:28-29	230
5:29b	230
17:24-25	42
17:24-28a	78, 170
20:21	226

ROMANS

1:16	226
1:16-17	212
3:23	73
8:24-25	244
8:26-27	83
8:37-39	240
10:1-3	48
11:33-36	60, 247
12:2	236
12:17-19	223
13:1-7	230
15:4	34, 135, 234
15:13	234
16:25-27	84, 100

1 CORINTHIANS

1:17	226
6:19-20	233
10:13	242
12:18-20	222
12:21-31	222
13:4-7	223
15:20-23	209
15:57-58	73, 101, 169

2 CORINTHIANS

2:14	17, 243
5:1-8	224
5:6-7	225
5:9-10	29, 97, 150
5:20	226

9:8-11	238
10:3-5	240
13:14	40, 80, 108, 133, 167

GALATIANS

6:1	223
6:14	47

EPHESIANS

1:7	229
1:17-19	67, 128
2:8-9	142, 184
2:19-22	26, 81
3:14-19	71, 132
3:20-21	92, 104
4:25-29	223
4:29-32	27, 124, 156
5:22-33	235
6:4	227
6:10-11	240
6:13-17	240
6:18-19	162
6:18-20	95, 141
6:19-20	152

PHILIPPIANS

1:6	225
1:9-11	75, 111
1:21-24	224
2:2-4	223
2:3-4	59, 151, 177
3:13-14	236

4:7	225
4:12-13	241
4:19	238

COLOSSIANS

1:9b-12	140
2:6-7	85
3:13	223
3:18-19	235
3:20-21	227
3:23-24	43, 137, 177
4:2-4	28, 161
4:2-6	152
4:5-6	19

1 THESSALONIANS

2:11-12	225
3:11-12	167, 183
3:11-13	75, 120
4:13-18	224
5:16-18	77
5:18	33, 138, 175, 243

2 THESSALONIANS

1:3	56
1:6-8	239
2:16-17	32, 72
3:1	137
3:1-3	237
3:3	240
3:5	115, 142, 156, 184

1 TIMOTHY

1:17	5
2:1-3	36
2:1-4	156, 178
3:4-5	227
4:4	243
4:8	233
5:8	227
6:17-19	232

2 TIMOTHY

2:11-13	58
2:19	90
3:16-17	34, 131, 155
4:5	226
4:7-8	23

TITUS

| 2:11-14 | 216 |
| 3:1 | 230 |

HEBREWS

1:3-4	97
4:1-3	239
4:8-11	239
4:14-16	182
6:19-20	234
10:23	234
10:24-25	225
10:25	222
11:1	234
12:1-3	241
13:2	40, 132

HEBREWS (CONTINUED)

13:2-3a	172
13:3	40, 132
13:7	222
13:16	44, 115, 167, 178
13:20-21	20, 48, 167

JAMES

1:12	242
4:7-8a	240
4:8-10	38
5:13-15	92, 233
5:16	5, 97
5:16b	221
5:16b-18	108
5:19-20	108

1 PETER

1:3-5	58, 123, 155
2:13-15	230
3:1-7	235
3:8-9	31, 115, 161, 183
3:8-11	223
5:8-9	240

2 PETER

1:19-21	38, 135, 160
3:8-9	244
3:8b-9	82

1 JOHN

1:8-9	41, 110, 159, 229
1:9-2:2	229, 242
4:4	225

3 JOHN

2	233

JUDE

20-23	100
24-25	24, 72, 116, 178

REVELATION

2:9-10	228
5:8	221
5:12b-13	45, 77
7:9-12	109
7:10b, 12b	76
8:3-4	221
14:13	224
15:3-4	147
19:6b-7, 9b	21
22:16b	21